Rural Communities

edited by
Yehuda H. Landau
Maurice Konopnicki
Henri Desroche
Placide Rambaud

Published in cooperation with
the Faculty of Social Sciences
of the University of Haifa
and the Settlement Study
Centre of Rehovot

The Praeger Special Studies program—
utilizing the most modern and efficient book
production techniques and a selective
worldwide distribution network—makes
available to the academic, government, and
business communities significant, timely
research in U.S. and international economic, social, and political development.

Rural Communities
Inter-Cooperation
and Development

Praeger Publishers New York Washington London

Library of Congress Cataloging in Publication Data
Main entry under title:

Rural communities.

  (Praeger special studies in international economics
and development)
    1. Community development—Addresses, essays, lectures.
2. Collective settlements—Israel—Addresses, essays,
lectures.   3. Agriculture, Cooperative—Addresses, essays,
lectures.   4. Villages—Addresses, essays, lectures.
I. Landau, Yehuda H., 1917-
HN49.C6R87   301.35   75-19779
ISBN 0-275-55700-6

PRAEGER PUBLISHERS
111 Fourth Avenue, New York, N.Y. 10003, U.S.A.

Published in the United States of America in 1976
by Praeger Publishers, Inc.

Printed in the United States of America

This book is based on the proceedings of the French-Israeli Conference on "Rural Communities—Inter-Cooperation and Development," which convened in Israel, Haifa and Rehovot, in the week of 13-18 May 1973, following the initiative of Henri Desroche during a visit to the University of Haifa and to the Settlement Study Centre of Rehovot. This interuniversity meeting, conceived within the France-Israeli cultural framework, grew from the close collaboration between the Centre de Récherches Coopératives (EPHE, Sorbonne), * the Faculty of Social Sciences of the University of Haifa, and the Settlement Study Centre of Rehovot.

After the opening session on May 13th at the University of Haifa, plenary sessions were held there on May 14th and 15th and at the Settlement Study Centre in Rehovot on May 18th, at which thirty-five papers were presented and discussed. May 16th and 17th were devoted to study tours to Galilee in the North and to the Lakhish Region in the South of Israel.

Due to technical limitations, we were obliged to select only fifteen out of the thirty-five papers presented at the Conference for translation and publication in this book, and even these had to be re-edited and condensed.

It is impossible to mention the long list of collaborators who contributed to the success of the Conference. We would like to give our warmest thanks to Henri Desroche, who initiated the idea of the Conference, accepted our invitation, and took a most active part in it, along with fifteen French, Belgian, Italian, and Spanish colleagues; to Zvi Sobel, Dean of the Faculty of Social Sciences of the University of Haifa, who gave priority to our project and offered us constant, decisive and unlimited support; to Eliezer Raphaeli, President of the University, who put at our disposal technical and administrative assistance in order to insure the success of our undertaking; to Raanan Weitz, Head of the Settlement Study Centre, who supported our project from start to finish; to Jean Soler, Cultural

---

*EPHE—Ecole Pratique des Hautes Etudes, now Ecole des Hautes Etudes en Sciences Sociales.

Attaché to the French Embassy in Tel-Aviv; to Abba Gefen, of the Israeli Ministry of Foreign Affairs; and to Yeshayahu Avreh of the Histadrut, who contributed to the success of the Conference.

We wish to emphasize the enormous amount of work carried by our two associates, Gaby Malka and Yossi Ambar, in the organization of the Conference.

Among the Israeli colleagues who joined us, the geographers played an essential part. We should like to express our thanks to Aharon Kellerman, Simon Stern, and Arnon Sofer, who offered to show us the country. Everyone agreed that these field-days were as interesting as those devoted to discussions. We shall never forget the wonderful welcome given to us at each stage of the journey. Many thanks to all those who received us so warmly in the regional centers of Milouot, Zemach, Nehora, and Schafir, at Kiryat Gat (Lakhish) and at the Kibbutz of Ein Gev and Merhavia.

CONTENTS

LIST OF TABLES AND FIGURE

INTRODUCTION
Maurice Konopnicki

The village as a basic development unit gives rise to innumerable reflections on training, stimulation, development, and communication phenomena in a rural environment. The study of the rural community assumes a more and more topical character within the scope of town-country relations in the unrestrained urbanization process we know today.

R. Ledrut[1] notes that at the beginning of the nineteenth century i all European and North American countries life in the countryside was intense and travellers found evidence of this vitality everywhere. The town has drawn amply on this source, developing its industries and waging its wars. The more the town prospered, the harder country life became; the capital represented by the soil depreciated, and the more capable men left it. The most important phenomenon was that the town appeared to be sapping its own base through the upsetting of the town-country equilibrium. How could it continue to subsist if there were no more farmers? How could it continue to develop without its demographic reserves?

The twentieth century town and civilization have taken up this challenge. Town-country relations are developing. The rural environment is now beginning to take a more prominent position. As a consequence of excessive industrialization and of the pollution and the aggressions of all kinds which attack the town dweller, there is a revival of interest in rural values. Many town dwellers believe they need the rural environment for their own happiness; they are aware that humanity cannot survive without it. Once merely a means of satisfying a more powerful class, the rural sector is now becoming a partner, not only in economic activities, but also in the search for quality in life.

No discernible improvement in the level of village life is resulting therefrom, however. The infatuation for the country shown by the town dweller appears to have had only marginal consequences on the farmers' economic and social situation. Moreover, in Europe the agricultural sector is constantly disturbed by manifestations, sometimes of a violent nature, of the uneasiness of the peasantry. The profound structural reforms considered by the Common Market (EEC) joint agricultural policy come up against the obtuseness and opposition of a population which is still insufficiently open to new techniques and methods. Everywhere, except for unusual cases such

as that of Israel, the standard of living in the rural sector is considerably lower than that in towns.

These problems no longer concern exclusively country people
since it has become obvious that the growth of world agriculture has
become problematic to an alarming extent since 1970. Will it be
possible to feed mankind in the year 2000? René Dumont warns that
while the production index per capita is stagnating in numerous
countries in Latin America and Africa, the specter of famine is re-
appearing and threatening millions of human beings. We are far from
the hopes expressed by the Food and Agricultural Organization (FAO)
planners who hoped to put an end to malnutrition by 1985.

> Famine is in our suburbs, but for a miracle. It is no
> longer the time to announce famine for tomorrow. It is
> more than ever omnipresent from the Andes to the North
> of Brazil, where the miracle is reserved for the rich,
> from Egypt to Iran, from Sahel to South-East Asia. In
> India, 60 percent of the rural population would appear to
> be living below the extreme poverty line. From Senegal
> to Chad, in this Spring of 1973, from India to Bangladesh,
> people are dying of hunger. [2]

Among the solutions proposed with a view to solving the difficulties of agricultural development there is one which sustains
attention because of its practically universal use: cooperation. Is
cooperation really a panacea capable of curing all the ills the agricultural world is suffering, and can it supply the Third World with
instruments for its development? Evidence, though contradictory,
is widely available, and shows the topical nature of the problem and
its acute character. While some writers devote all their efforts to
extreme praise of the success of cooperation, increasing numbers
of them are asking questions and are constructively criticizing the
principles of cooperation and their application in the rural sector
for the benefit, not of the cooperative theory itself, but of the
prosperity of the whole community.

Many people question the form taken by state intervention in
favor of agricultural cooperation and its expedience. [3] Some recent
works stand out by virtue of their critical nature and their contribution to a better knowledge of the mechanics of relations between
agricultural cooperation and the state. J. Berthelot[4] and L. E.
Bourgeois[5] emphasize the ambiguity of state agricultural cooperation relations, especially in France.

The United Nations Institute for Social Development (UNRISD)
offers a series of reports on cooperatives and rural development

throughout the world, from which emerges, particularly in O. Fals Borda's[6] study on Latin America, a critique of traditional concepts of cooperation, deemed to be inapplicable to developing countries.

In the Common Market (EEC), the prosperity of the agricultural cooperatives which appears to be suggested in the evolution of statistical data in fact dissimulates in certain regions a very considerable deterioration in the condition of the peasantry. The first point to be noted is the ambiguity of the definitions. Cooperatives display their statutes with the sole aim of making profit, while the behavior of their members is completely alien to the cooperative spirit. "In fact, many cooperatives are very rapidly 'assimilated.' Seeking at the same time no longer to differ from the surrounding environment and to get protection from the authorities, by claiming to be non-profitmaking undertakings, they have often obtained certain privileges and exemptions to laws applicable to 'the others'".[7]

Moreover, the biggest cooperative units and the most competitive in face of the capitalist sector show a considerable distortion of cooperative law leading to a domination by the cooperative management over the members. Deviations are particularly noted at management and decision-making levels which no longer have any democratic character. The increasing contradictions existing between the non-capitalist aims of the cooperative management and the competitive relations being established on the market with capitalist enterprises lead to the dominance of the wage-earning executives of the management committee over members.

In spite of the numerous privileges from which they benefit in France (at tax, social, financial, and insurance levels), the management of French cooperatives often appears less efficient than that of private enterprises.

The increasing support offered by the state and the "Crédit Agricole" appears to lead to a process of servitude of the cooperatives. Indeed the assistance afforded comprises a more and more encroaching power exerted by those authorities over the direction of growth of the cooperative. This process tends to take out of the farmers' hands the real control of cooperative capital and leads finally to capitalist-type relations between the cooperative and a considerable portion of its members.

This excessive solicitude on the part of French legislators towards agricultural cooperatives takes away from them a part of their will to exercise initiatives and is also reflected in the too frequent modifications to the statutes. The believers in cooperative orthodoxy appeal to Charles Gide[8] who strongly stated that "a true cooperative movement must walk by itself and not with the crutches supplied to it by the state." This extremely rigorous conception

denouncing recourse to state intervention appears to be partly questioned
in developing countries. Present everywhere in developing countries,
the cooperative sees its coming into being keenly encouraged by international organizations such as the FAO or the ILO. Training and
technical assistance implements have also been set up in a large
number of developing countries. In Africa particularly, there are innumerable training centers of this kind. Such actions, whose merits
appear to be recognized by a considerable number of developing
countries, do not however, after many years' experience, show surpassing (lasting) results. The rare statistical data hardly seem to bear
witness to prosperity on the part of agricultural cooperation. It must
also be recognized that the figures have only a problematical statistical value, since numerous companies counted are cooperative only
in name.

A new fact has recently come to light in the literature on cooperation in developing countries: "Condemnation of the Cooperative
Illusion," a severe criticism of cooperation, which is unfit to play
its part as promoter with regard to the poor peasantry.[9] Whereas
certain purists condemned by D. L. W. Anker devote considerable time
to questioning themselves on the authenticity of certain forms of cooperation,[10] wrongly considered as a panacea in the matter of rural
development, a specialist on African problems deplores the ill-
considered use of cooperative terminology: "Cooperation has been
invited or imported into Africa as, for example, something capable
of transcending at the same time capitalism and socialism, while
being an instrument for the one and an enemy for the other. Cooperation is held to be the same policy which brought about social
changes in Africa as in Europe, in the colonial as well as in the post-
colonial period. Cooperation affirmed in such general terms, even
when limited to an agricultural or rural sector, belongs to that same
order of illusions as the idea of utopia. This may serve the interests
of demagogues and tyrants, and of a bureaucracy whose salaried
members depend on the continuance of the status quo for their incomes
and security...."[11]

Criticism becomes final condemnation where the application of
so-called cooperative methods in a Latin-American rural environment
is concerned. E. Feder[12] attributes the failure of the action of the
cooperatives in Latin America to the fundamental contradiction between the basic principles of cooperation and the political, economic
and social structure of Latin American society. Authentic cooperation is actually considered as being subversive there, and does not
enjoy the political support of national or local governments, of the
church, or of the local elite, since it defies the existing social regime.

How, then, have cooperatives been able to survive? Fundamentally by agreeing to concessions to the authorities in power. In many cases equality between members is nothing but a snare, with the cooperatives often coming to reflect the society in which they operate. In reality these cooperatives will often be managed by members of the community who stand out through their political, economic, and social power, including rich landowners, tradesmen, and bankers. Consequently, the cooperative becomes an instrument intended to perpetuate the commercial interests of powerful local elements. When the cooperatives threaten to become prosperous, powerful forces are set to work with a view to undermine their activities.

Confirming the preceding views, O. Fals Borda[13] also expresses in the bitterest terms his disappointment of the failure of the Latin American cooperatives and the gravity of the consequences: "Never a day passes, without—here or there—a Latin American cooperative closing its doors, with all that this implies in the way of wasted resources, blighted hopes and disappointments."

However, in spite of this long series of frustrations and setbacks, it is strange to note that cooperativism remains the cornerstone of the social policy of many governments. It is true that the latent function of this cooperativism is the maintaining of the status quo. The ultimate aim is not so much to favor the autonomy of the rural classes as to maintain bonds of subordination within a renovated framework. O. Fals Borda considers, in addition, that the appeal to an old ideal of cooperation, out of date and alien to the area, is, in a society dominated by paternalism and exploitation, conceived as a diversion maneuver against the working-classes of the population. Generally speaking, the cooperatives have not broadened the political and civic consciousness of their members and have not stimulated in a significant way self-determination, autonomy, and a creative spirit among the peasantry. Any attempt at a real educational campaign undertaken by a cooperative constitutes an intolerable challenge to the system and will be nipped in the bud, as will any development which tends towards more active participation of the members and thus risks a redistribution of wealth.

A. P. Laidlaw[14] supports the primary of the role of the government in the matter of cooperation in developing countries. According to him, in practically all these countries the form taken by the cooperatives and the way in which they are organized and developed depends largely on government policy and on the work of its officials. In fact the political atmosphere generally prevents any significant development of the cooperatives outside government initiatives.

In a masterful analysis of the relations between the state and agricultural cooperation in French-speaking countries in Black Africa, Andre Hirschfeld[15] presents a particularly moderate view of the question.

Public authorities, over and above their legislative or statutory work, have very often granted to agricultural cooperatives in French-speaking Black Africa considerable financial aid in various forms and on repayment terms very favorable to them. State intervention has also manifested itself by the granting of a privileged tax regime, by permitting monopolies of certain cooperative operations, and by the establishment and financing of education in cooperation (initiation of the lower ranks, or even sometimes higher education for the staff of cooperatives). A. Hirschfeld considers this intervention indispensable, since the assumption of responsibility by the populations concerned, without assistance and control by government, appears premature. The self-management of new economic structures is conditioned by a process of learning, adjustment, and change of ancestral habits. Moreover, in countries in which the market is dominated by enterprises with profit-making aims which are under the control of very powerful national or international companies, complete independence of the cooperative movement presents great dangers.

The conclusions of an inquiry carried out in 14 rural communities in Ceylon, Iran, and Pakistan[16] express exactly the same view. In these cooperatives there is no evidence of resentment expressed by leaders or members towards supervision and intervention by local officials. The cooperative is considered a government agency and consequently the control exercised by inspectors and official departments constitutes a normal and legitimate procedure. For many, especially the leaders, the fear of intervention by officials was most probably the main reason they did not misuse the resources of the cooperative.

Y. Levi[17] also emphasizes the gaps caused by too great government solicitude: adoption of policies insuring the continuation of the colonial period, limitation of foreign legislative texts inadequately adapted to local requirements, excessive investment weakening local initiative by accustoming it to having recourse to outside aid, inadequacy of education efforts prior to the setting up of the cooperatives, and a tendency to accelerate the setting up of a large number of cooperatives.

Another concept, one which rejects the traditional forms of technical assistance and the classical models of rural development through the formulas of the cooperation movement, sustains attention: self-development, or the absolute necessity of stimulating and encouraging among rural populations in developing countries initiatives directed

at adapting cooperative formulas to their own culture, social organization and structure. This theme of self-development has been approached
by several participants in our Conference who reviewed experiences
of development from below and offered samples of social creative-
ness: in France, the establishment of a collective will through the
initiative of local innovators; in the Spanish Basque area, the Mon-
dragon industrial complex, the cooperative initiative was taken by a
few private individuals; in Brittany, particular characteristics inspired original cooperative models; in the South Sea Islands, the
emergence of indigenous development gave rise to decision-making
without the intervention of outside factors; in Israel, practically all
the cooperative system in rural areas was born of initiatives coming
from below and at present, the Kibbutz and the Moshav are at a high
level of development in agriculture as well as in industry and are
characterized by a constant search for new ways of action.

There comes a time when, in the course of social and economic
progress, various forms of cooperation must be linked   (consumption,
industrial production, credit, and agriculture for example) to whatever the population may be (peasantry, workmen, savers, consumers)
and, over and above particular local characteristics, to regional or
even interregional associations. This theme of intercooperation is
particularly in evidence in Brittany and Israel, where numerous manifestations of these links tend to interweave and form an extremely
close-knit unit favorable to development.

In Israel regional cooperation in rural areas is manifested by
the setting up of rural service centers which have the specific merit
of facilitating the integration of groups of different ethnological origins.

Although the disparities between population groups of differing
ethnological origins in Israel have not disappeared, and although they
are particularly evident in the appearance of unprivileged social classes
in urban environments, it should be emphasized that the high standard
of living in the rural sector tends to reduce such disparities amongst
village populations.

The pooling of resources with a view to meeting the requirements of technological progress, the increase in farmers' income
through the setting up of regional enterprises and agricultural processing industries, and the creation of nonagricultural jobs are some
of the advantages offered to the Israeli rural community by inter-
cooperation. However, this regional cooperation is not always
achieved without friction. Economic change is often accompanied by
serious social conflicts which may endanger fundamental ideological
principles.

It would appear that other and more diversified sources of
income will have to be added to the activities centered on cultivating

the soil, which make use of less and less manual labor. Village communities could attain at the same time a post-village society and a post-industrial society, in which town-country discrimination would be absorbed and where, within an ecological setting of the primary sector, facilities of the secondary and tertiary sectors would be implanted—village areas in which the working populations would be increasingly engaged in agricultural activities, although such areas would remain societies with village populations.

Developing countries in which the notion of the rural cooperative community, as distinct from that of rural cooperatives, represents an instrument for development of an economic society, were of special interest to the participants in the discussion. An original model of rural cooperative communities presented by Y. Levi goes beyond the mere granting of cooperative services. This model suggests ways to overcome the problems of adaptability and of the inadequacy of classical cooperation in rural areas in less developed countries. The least costly and most positive experiments were those in which the peasantry themselves decided on the program to be followed and the scale on which it was to be carried out. The multiplying of small local projects, accessible to a fairly considerable number of individuals, will permit the adhesion of the latter to the actual taking over of the structures thus set up. The grafting on of outside elements, even with the best of intentions, will most often be rejected. Although formal cooperatives should generally be encouraged, in individual cases an alternative organization should be permitted. Cooperatives should be made as attractive as possible, but not by creating unrealistic expectations of them, or by artificial constraints on other forms of business organization.

We conclude this survey of the main themes approached with some fundamental questions put by Gaston Lanneau:[18] "Why and how does a farmer become a cooperator? What are the meanings and implications of his adhesion?"

It is noted that it is essentially during periods in which the balance of economic and social structures is threatened or destroyed that the system of relations founded on work is itself affected, and that new forms of cooperation appear, progress, and spread.

Cooperation can be considered as an answer to a threat born of society; it is reflected by a strengthening of the overall cohesion of the farmers when the danger comes from outside, and by a splitting up of that cohesion when that threat is both exogenous and endogenous. Mutual aid is a defense against elements, such as isolation or atmospheric agents which may be mitigated by associating with our fellowmen who are in a similar situation. The farmer has recourse to others when the strain brought about by the gap between the strength

necessary to satisfy his needs and that which he has available reaches
a certain level. The final aim of cooperation is the transformation of
conditions of life, some only related to the purely economic aspects,
others to social and psychological needs as well, thus favoring the
qualitative aspect.

The extremely detailed psychological analysis of G. Lanneau
discerns three phases of cooperation: a state of absence of differentiation manifested by mutual aid; a phase of differentiation characterized
by the increase of specialized forms of cooperation; and finally, a
phase of unification, integration, and synthesis, during which an
attempt is made to unify what had been dislocated during the preceding
phase.

NOTES

1. Raymond Ledrut, "La croissance urbaine facteur de muta-
tion," in Sociological mutations (Paris: Editions Anthropos, 1970),
291-300.

2. R. Dumont, "Nous allons a la famine" (Paris: Ed. du Seuil,
1970); "L'utopie ou la mort" (Paris: Ed. du Seuil, 1973).

3. M. Konopnicki, "Co-opération agricole et l'État", in
Annales de l'économie publique, sociale et co-opérative no. 1
(Liège, 1975): 55-80.

4. J. Berthelot, Les co-opératives agricoles en économie
concurrentielle (Paris: Cujas, 1972).

5. E. Bourgeois, La co-opérative agricole face aux problemes
de commercialisation (Paris: Cufas, 1967).

6. O. Fals Borda, R. Inayatullah, ed. Apthorpe, United Nations
Research Institute for Social Development, Rural Institutions and
Planned Change, Geneva, 1970-72, volumes 1-7: A Review of Rural
Cooperation in Developing Areas; Estudios de la realidad campesina:
cooperacion y cambio; Cooperatives and Rural Development in Latin
America: an Analytic Report; Rural Cooperatives and Planned Change
in Africa: Case Materials; Rural Cooperatives and Planned Change in
Africa: An Analytical Overview; Cooperatives and Planned Change in
Asian Rural Countries; and Cooperatives and Development in Asia:
A Study of Cooperatives in 14 Rural Communities of Iran, Pakistan,
and Ceylon.

7. R. Louis, "Reflexions sur certains problèmes posés par la
législation co-opérative", Informations Co-operatives no. 1, (Geneva:
Bureau International du Travail, 1975): 49.

8. Charles Gide, "La co-opération dans les pays latins", Associations pour l'enseignement de la co-opération, Paris 1927.

9. Y. Goussault, "Stratifications sociales et co-opération agricole" in "Le développement rural", Revue Tiers-Monde (Paris: Presses Universitaires de France, April-June 1973): 281-82.

10. D. L. W. Anker, "Le développement rural. Problèmes et Plans d'action," in Révue international du travail 108, no. 6 (Geneva: December 1973): 509-10.

11. R. Apthorpe, "Some Problems of Evaluation in Carl Gosta Widstrand-Cooperatives and Rural Development in East Africa," The Scandinavian Institute for African Studies (New York: Upsala, and The African Publishing Corporation, 1970), p. 211.

12. E. Feder, "Solving the Problems of Production, Unemployment and Poverty—Dilemma facing Agricultural Co-operatives in Latin America," paper presented at the International Symposium "Dynamics of Interrelations between Agricultural Co-operatives and the Government," Tel Aviv, 1974.

13. O. Fals Borda, "Formation et déformation de la politique co-opérative en Amérique latine," Informations co-opératives (Geneva: Bureau International du Travail, 1970); and "Co-operatives and Rural Development in Latin America, An Analytic Report," in Rural Institutions and Planned Change (Geneva: UNRISD, 1971).

14. A.F. Laidlaw, "Mobilization of Human Resources for Rural Development Through Agricultural Co-operatives" (Rome: FAO): 23-25.

15. A. Hirschfeld, report presented at the Tel Aviv Symposium, "État et co-opération agricole en Afrique noire francophones," Revue des études co-opératives no. 177, (Paris: March 1974): 25-46.

16. Inayatullah, "Co-operatives and Development in Asia—A Study of Co-operation in 14 Rural Communities of Iran, Pakistan and Ceylon," (Geneva: UNRISD, 1972): 253-54.

17. Y. Levi, "The Co-operative Dilemma in Rural Developing Areas: Development 'From Below' or 'From Above'," paper presented at the International Symposium (Tel Aviv: 1974).

18. G. Lanneau, "Essai d'Analyse Psycho-Sociologique des Fondements de la Co-opération Agricole," Archives Internationales de Sociologie de la Co-operation et du Développement no. 36 (July-December 1974): 22-46. See also G. Lanneau, "Agriculture et Co-opération", Archives Internationales de Sociologie de la Co-operation et du développement no. 25 (Paris: January-June 1969): 131-200.

I

VILLAGE ASSOCIATION
AND RURAL DEVELOPMENT

DEVELOPMENT FROM BELOW
AND INTER-COOPERATION
OF RURAL COMMUNITIES
Henri Desroche

Over the last decade a series of conferences has been held in conjunction with our Israeli colleagues with discussion centered on themes related to those under consideration in this publication.[1]

In addition, Israeli villages and their intervillage institutions have been the object of a great deal of research available in the French language.[2]

CENTRE DE RÉCHERCHES COOPÉRATIVES

Our Centre de Récherches Coopératives annually allocates about a hundred postgraduate students to research projects which are generally based on professional experience in village or intervillage development, with special emphasis on cooperative or intercooperative aspects. The three main sociological subjects represented in their work are:

Rural Sociology

Colloquia held at Albiez-le Vieux's (1970-71) dealt with villages of France, Africa, and Madagascar, Europe and the Middle East, and Asia and Latin America. This first series of publications has been followed by bibliographical surveys.[3] In his introduction P. Rambaud raises a question related to our theme: "Rural space may become an important element for non-farming activities. Will urban development not make it increasingly necessary to rely on a social and spatial organization different from that of the cities?"[4,5]

Rural development appears to bring together two forces: one of decentralization based on micro-regionalization; the other of aggregation of dispersed groupings. This second tendency has given rise to various experiments in African countries such as "communes of development" in Senegal[6] the regrouping of villages in Nigeria[7], and the Zones d'Action Prioritaires Integrées (ZAPI) in the Cameroons.[8] The search has been for optimum economies of scale for a "unit of development" in which optimum social participation can be achieved.

Sociology of Cooperation

The approach of village societies to cooperative development implies the recurrence of a century-old problem of European origin. The cooperative movement originated in utopian ideals of English, French, and German thinkers, aiming at creating communal societies such as the "Harmony Villages" of the Owenites. This is illustrated by the "First Law" of the Rochdale pioneers. In France the Icariens (1860) saw cooperation as "the system of transition best suited to prepare us for communal life." Later Charles Gide paid tribute to these nostalgic ideals[9], and since Gide, they have erupted frequently, as in the wave of French "Work Communes" of twenty-five years ago; and in the present-day wave of "Youth Communes."[10]

Despite such nostalgia for multifunctional communes, the classic development of the cooperative has almost everywhere been along single purpose lines, such as consumers' cooperatives, workers' cooperatives for industrial production, farmers' agricultural cooperatives, or credit cooperatives of savings societies. Thus the development of the cooperative has closely followed that of commercial, industrial, agricultural, and banking enterprises without identifying with them ecologically or sociologically speaking. This scheme of things is put into question by R. Weitz's new strategy of development, which calls for the integration of human, social, and geographical functions into a multifunctional focus which serves cooperative purposes. This focus, sought first in the utopian microcommune, then in the ideological macrorepublic (the cooperative republic), later limited to a specific economic sector (the 'cooperative' sector), is now found to be located in economic-ecological complexes, which are neither utopian nor ideological, nor exclusively economic. It is with this problem that our symposium is concerned.

Andragogic Sociology

This refers to a type of change particularly found in developing countries and regions. It occurs in village societies which reluctantly

admit change, but which consider that if change must come it should
not be unilateral. Andragogy, as UNESCO has styled it, is of fundamental importance in counteracting satellization and alienation. It
marshals all forces of animation, information, formation, promotion,
and participation at its disposal in order to save human liberty from
the encroachment of economic determinism. The urgent attention paid
to the environmental problems in recent years has also had an influence in resisting unilateral "developmentism" that extends to the
educational crisis of our time.[11]

PROSPECTS

The following four working hypotheses arise from our investi-
gations in Israel, as well as from other comparative research projects.

Development from Below- a Postulate

From the discussions on principles of cooperation held at the
International Cooperative Alliance (ICA) congresses in 1934 and 1937
and at the Congress of Vienna in 1966 there emerges an attitude of an
economic ethic, traditionally known as "self help" and "mutual aid,"
and which we call here "development from below."
    An old French association dating back to the year 1840 adopted
as its slogan the saying, "Heaven helps those who help themselves."
"Heaven" certainly has not failed the Cooperative Movement in its
more spectacular achievements, although we have all witnessed
certain signs of disintegration when the process of grafting—technical
or financial—has been rejected by the organism.
    Max Weber demonstrated the interaction between ethical attitude
and economic behaviour[12], with the example of the Calvinist ethic
and its bearing on capitalist enterprise and entrepreneur. A parallel
is to be found not only in non-European regions, as Eisenstadt suggests, but in eras other than the capitalist era. Francois Perroux,
the economist, has indicated a parallel of this kind which he calls the
"Saint-Simonism of the twentieth century" in describing collective
creation or creativity. Not even planned development dispenses with
creativity of this kind. As the Russian economist Tchayanov once
wrote, "The art of planning is not in the drawing of the plan but in
giving it life."[13] There is no development without development from
below, that is to say, without inventive economic creativity involving
men and means.

An Institution: Cooperation as an Intra-Village Institution

The observation of Israeli villages reveals the danger of making over-simplified classifications, such as "cooperative farming" or "family farming." The "moshav" and the "kibbutz" offer models of an adjustment between economic performance and social preference, with the "moshav shitufi" playing the transitional role. To these must be added many other social patterns, like the Yugoslav general cooperative, delicately balanced between the zadrouga and the economy[14], the Mexican Ejidos[15], the Chilean assentamiento, the Algerian self-management sector[16], and the kolkhoz [17]. Many institutional varieties of intra-village cooperation exist. We must avoid the temptation of classifying them too narrowly, according to criteria of good or bad. [18]

A Constraint: Cooperation as an Inter-village Institution

Whatever the internal model of a village cooperative may be, it is influenced by certain external factors such as the supply of material and equipment for production and the distribution and commercialization of the produce. The village has to be regarded as a miniature fusé to which are attached multiple wires that lead to the various devices and means through which it functions. No village development can evade inter-village integration. The villages either develop and go along with it or become subordinate to it.

Two types of inter-village integration, ascending and descending, are discernible; one is an economic integration of agricultural production and the other is an ecological integration of the village community. The Israeli experience offers us two cases in point: the "Irgunei Kniot," or Purchasing Organizations, and the Regional Councils for Development.

A Utopia: the Dawn of a Meta-Urban, Meta-Rural Society

We have been warned about the utopian type of socialization by two classic figures of "scientific" socialism, Marx and Engels. We find written in the Manifesto of 1848: "the combination of agricultural and industrial labour will gradually lead to a disappearance of the distinction between town and country." "The greatest difference between material labour and spiritual labour is to be found in the comparative condition of town and country." "The first great division of labour, the schism between town and country has destroyed the basis of intellectual development for some, and that of physical development for others." "The elimination of the conflict between town and country is not merely a possibility, it has become a necessity."

Optimistic as this outlook may be—and reminiscent as it is of Bismarck's "the death of large towns"—it reinforces our working hypothesis. It bears within it the seeds of paradox, a fact brought out by reference to the investigation presently being carried out on the eventual development of the Rwandian shores of Lake Kivu. [19] It is no fantasy, however, as is demonstrated by the obstinacy with which rural Israel has absorbed within its primary sector factors already deeply implanted in the second or third, such as kibbutz industrialization; supply and services offered by such inter-village institutions as the Purchasing Organization or the Regional Development Council. The underlying hypothesis is neither a kind of fixation nor a return "to the soil," but, on the contrary, takes into account the ubiquitous decrease of the population actively engaged in agricultural production. The population released in this way is not, however, involved in any kind of geographic mobility. It is rather that secondary and tertiary types of technology are conscripted from the urban to the rural areas to satisfy the new kind of demands for employment. Ideally, the transplanted elements, whether of industry, supply, or services, should arise out of a combination of development from below and intercooperation. There is hope that this will be achieved as a result of advances in inter-mediate technology, a field in which many laboratories are actively engaged at the present time.

NOTES

1. Colloque de Paris, Planification et Volontariat dans les Développements Coopératifs (Paris: La Haye, Mouton, 1962); Colloque de Tel-Aviv 1965, The Role of Cooperation in Rural Development, Tel Aviv, C.I.R.C.O.M., 2 vol.; Coopération Agricole et Développement Rural (Paris: La Haye, Mouton, 1966); Colloque de Tel-Aviv 1969, ed. by J. Klatzmann and Y. Levy, The Role of Group Action in the Industrialization of Rural Areas (New York and London: Praeger, 1971); Colloques d'Albiez le Vieux, 1970-71, ed. by H.D. and P. Rambaud, Villages en Développement. Contribution à une Sociologie Villageoise (Paris: La Haye, Mouton, 1972).

2. H. Desroche and Gat, Z., Opération Mochav. D'un Développement des Villages à une villagisation du développement (Paris: Cufas, 1973); H. Desroche, Au Pays du Kibboutz, in essay on the Israeli Cooperative Sector (Bale: Union Suisse des Cooperatives de Consommation, 1960); J. Shatil, L'Économie Collective du Kibboutz Israélien (Paris: Minuit, 1962); L. Szeskin, Les Trois Secteurs Industriels de l'Économie Ouvrière Israélienne, Cahier du Centre de

Recherches Cooperatives, no. 17 (Paris: Bureau D'Etudes Coopératives et Communautaires, 1964); A. Meister, Principes et Tendances
de la Planification Rurale en Israël (Paris: La Haye, Mouton, 1962);
C. Lambert, Un Mochav au Negueb (Paris: Bureau D'Etudes Coopéra-
tives et Communautaires, 1959); R. Janover, L'Intégration des Juifs
Tunisiens en Israël: le Mochav Yanouv (Paris: Ecole Pratique des
Hautes Etudes, 1970); J. Klatzmann, Les Enseignements de l'Expéri-
ence Israélienne (Paris: Presses Universitaires de France, 1963);
E. Desroche, "Le Mochav Chitoufi ou Kibboutz Familial" (Paris:
Ecole Pratique des Hautes Etudes, 19 72), published in part as
"Coopération et Mutualité au Mochav Chitoufi," Archives Internationales
de Sociologie de la Coopération et du Developpement 32; M. Konopnicki,
La Coopération en Milieu Rural Israëlien (Liège: La Haye, Martinus
Nuhoff, 1968); A. Daniel, La coopération de production et de services
en Israël (Paris, 1963); H. Infield, Coopératives communautaires et
sociologie expérimentale. Esquisse d'une sociologie de la coopération
(Paris: Minuit, 1956); I. Guelfat, La Coopération devant la Science
Économique (Paris: PUF, 1966); H. Darin Drapkin, The Other Society,
(London: Gollencz, 1962). In French, Le Kibboutz, Sociéte Différente
(Paris: Seuil, 1970); H. Infield, Cooperative Living in Palestine (London:
Kegan Paul, 1946); R. Weitz, From Peasant to Farmer, A Revolu-
tionary Strategy for Development (New York and London: Columbia
University Press, 1971).

    3. B. Kerblay, "La sociologie du village soviétique", AISCD, 32
(1972): pp. 112-174, and Sur le village suisse, to be published by S.
Zurini in AISCD, 33.

    4. Kerblay, op. cit.

    5. The question is further complicated by a twofold movement:
the mobility of people engaged in agriculture is mainly from village to
town, but there also exists a movement from town to village, either as
a result of people returning to the village or of people moving to the
country following changes in the image of the village among town
dwellers. See also our introduction to M. Vincienne,Du village a la
ville (The Hague: Mouton, 1972).

    6. P. Laville, Associations paysannes et socialisme contractuel
en Afrique de l'Ouest. A case study (Senegal and Paris: Cufas, 1972).

    7. G. Belloncle, Expérience et animation coopérative au Niger
(Paris: BECC, 1966); and Pedagogie de l'Implantation du Mouvement
Cooperatif au Niger (Paris: BECC, 1969).

    8. J. Lenglart, Les zones d'actions prioritaires integrées
(ZAPI) de l'Est Cameroun (Paris: Diplome EPHE, 1972), p. 470.

    9. C. Gide, Les colonies communistes et coopératives (Paris:
Association pour L'Enseignement de la Cooperation, 1928).

10. See the contributions of D. Leger, "Le Développement des communautés de base en France," AISCD 31 (1972): pp. 23-48, and J. Seguy, "Notes sur les communes américaines", AISCD 33.

11. An exhaustive list of papers in French on this subject, a bibliographic review of some 6000 titles of books, articles, and documents has been prepared by our Centre in collaboration with the Canadian Institute for Adult Education (Montreal). See P. Richard and P. Paquet, "L'Éducation permanente et ses concepts périphériques," (Paris: Cujas, 1973), AISCD 32.

12. It has been our privilege to publish a paper by our colleague from Jerusalem, S. Eisenstadt, "Some Reflections on the Significance of Max Weber's Sociology of Religions for the Analysis of Non-European Modernity," in the Archives de Sociologie des Réligions 32 (July-December, 1972): pp. 29-52.

13. Quoted and commented upon by B. Kerblay in Cahiers du Monde Russe et Soviétique (October-December, 1964).

14. Not to speak of the further complication introduced by the entry of the self-development Kombinat. See our article: "Combinat et Zadrouga. Industrialization autogestionnaire et paysannerie co-opérative in Yougoslavie," AISCD 29 (January-June 1971): pp. 3-88.

15. H. Infield, People in Ejidos (New York: Praeger, 1955); Eckstein, S., El Ejido Colectivo en México (Mexico: Fodo de Cultural Económica, 1966).

16. S. Koulytchisky, "Dynamiques de l'autogestion. Genese et ambivalence de l'expérience Algérienne," AISCD 31 (1972): 131-83.

17. B. Kerblay, "Le nouveau statut des Kolkhozes", AISCD 26: 179-88.

18. M. Bloch, Apologie pour l'histoire du métier d'historien (Paris: Colin, 1961), pp. 70-71.

19. C.I.N.A.M., Étude du développement de la région du Lac Kivu, 3 vols. (March 1973).

2

VILLAGE AND COOPERATIVE
AGRICULTURE OF FRANCE
Placide Rambaud

At present the village is considered as a typical unit of anti -
development, in France at any rate. Its small size, its traditions,
its conflicts, connected often with demographic impoverishment, and
its generally uniform agrarian economy all invest it with the immobil-
ity with which it faces the insurgent forces of town and industry. Nevertheless, it exhibits astonishing tenacity, dynamic and imaginative to a
high degree. There are numerous attempts at new forms of spatial and
social organization that may redesign industrialized societies. In the
village the agricultural cooperative has introduced a singular form of
development, covering everything from economic affairs to decision-
making, from political relations to cultural interests. In all this, constraints of agrarian individualism are felt which, although they have
undermined the old communal customs, have not managed to destroy
their foundations, or the need for them. Cooperative initiative seems
to present a juxtaposition here: while not taking over entirely, and
being limited to only a few people, it has almost imperceptibly in-
jected into the village a powerful dynamism which ultimately modifies
its most entrenched traditions, as a new economic force which pits
its power with ease against that of the older communal one.

THE CONSTRAINTS OF AGRARIAN INDIVIDUALISM

France is not only the country of villages, but also the country
of agrarian individualism, psychological as well as structural. It
consists of a web of 33,656 rural communities with an average of
450 inhabitants having at their disposal 1,340 hectares. If, as in the

case of the "buraku" of Japan, the hamlet is considered the primary
unit, and if each commune consists of at least five hamlets, then
France is organically fragmented into some 170,000 villages, each
containing 85 inhabitants forming about fifteen families. There are
about 1,587,470 agricultural units, 47 for each commune, consisting
of 20.5 hectares each; in actual fact about half can only cultivate
less than ten hectares. These units are a mosaic of fragmented plots,
70 million in all, 12 to each owner, about 40 to each enterprise; the
average area of a cadastral unit is about 42 ares (4,200 square meters).
This individualistic type of structure has a bearing on all agricultural
undertakings and policies.

The village is predominately a kinship group, an agrarian economy
and localy polity with consolidated but at times aggressive tendencies.
There is a long-established communal sense of collective ownership
of certain public property and the enjoyment of equal rights which makes
for economic opportunity equally open to all, with no private benefit
tolerated. When any imported activity such as tourism intervenes,
there takes place a vigorous and interested resurgence of the sense of
communal ownership and usage, ensuring that this communal sense,
which should operate in the protection of the poor, does not merely
serve as a means of expansion for the rich. This is coupled with a
second characteristic, arising from the permanent, rigorous application of the principle of local autonomy which designates as "foreign"
anyone who is not part of the well defined society. The village is dis-
tinguished by a system of communication and exchange which is economic and informative, political and critical, distrustful and emotional,
mainly regulated by kinship considerations. This arises from the fact
that its constituent elements are families, or rather, family farms.
They are at the root of all initiatives and the power of communal
decision-making emanates from their common will, even if it is
always provisional and conflicting. This common basis is the source
of all development.

The commune insures, or perpetually re-establishes, the cohesion and equilibrium of the local unit, which patterns of family relationships establish or disturb in accordance with their own peculiar
logic. It is in this way that the commune controls village sociability
and antagonism, a function linked to political action, where the lines
of kinship relations are always evident. Land ownership and family
alliances combine to make political action subservient to kinship
organization. It should be easy to expose the conservative impact of
these family ramifications in all their density, consolidated as they
are in perpetuity of ownership; however, there are no studies to show
how kinship attempts to domesticate communal politics and how the
decline of the former opens new horizons for the latter. The commune

consists of individuals who are unequal by birth and property but who
are all considered as equal before the law. In endowing them with the
same rights and obligations, this equality is both protective and ab-
stract. Thus the commune as such ignores the concept of worker, that
is, the farm as a working group, and in so doing, an important part
of the economy and of the village. As a result of this dual disregard,
the commune does not function so as to evolve an economic policy,
even if it manages the communal property (10% of the land) and controls its collective use, sometimes even organizing the latter in cooperative fashion.

FROM INDIVIDUALISM TO AGRARIAN COOPERATIVE ENTERPRISE

Until recently, cooperative enterprise in agriculture has stood
side by side with legal and rigid individual cultivation. Through it,
the farmers expect mainly to find new ways to organize their economic relations of purchasing and marketing with industrialized society
This was first codified and thus publicly encouraged after the major
crisis of the years 1880-1900. Cooperatives for collection, processing
and marketing have been established whose status has gradually adapted
to changes in the economy. Today there are 5,073 cooperatives, four
out of ten have less than one hundred active members. They bring
together 3,600,000 registered members, only two-thirds of whom are
active. In a second phase starting around 1945, another initiative, the
work cooperative, developed. It transformed the statute, the organization, and the powers of decision-making of the family farm as the result of change in the social aspects of labor.

The marketing cooperative is a way of fighting the stringent
demands of the economy by concentrating supply or demand, but only
at the level of the market. The study of cooperative organisms shows
that they are most frequently the result of a commercial crisis. Small
dairies or wine producers are a perfect example. Completely integrated into the village, these cooperatives offer a solution to a local
problem of processing or marketing. The distances and means of
transport available and the degree of mutual understanding and confidence in the neighborhood dictate the small size of units. Their
function is strictly commercial, which is the reason they are always
specialized. They are service cooperatives, and as the name indicates they are simply an extension of the family farm, utilized by the
farmer when it suits him, discarded in favor of private dealers when
it does not. They don't have a specific economic project of their own,
only that of their members.

The absence of a wider economic goal does not mean that this type of cooperative is in any way inefficacious. In the first place, it has been the means of instituting a new kind of sociability in the village. Also, in concentrating the supply or demand it has consolidated agrarian individualism by increasing its income and strengthening its structure. While perpetuating the logic of the individual farm it protects it against the over-abusive domination of private commerce. Its dual origin, the individualism of farming and the swift reaction to dissatisfactions caused by private dealers, explains its recent evolution. These cooperatives are becoming less and less guided by the needs of the farmers in their effort to become more competitive.

The effort to prove competitive as regards the private sector, in the interests of agriculture as opposed to aggressive capitalism, has inspired a second and rather less village-like type of commercial cooperative. The growth in production and the gainful possibilities offered by the interest of industry in agricultural production have increased the disparity between different products and even between regions. This has obliged the cooperatives to model their activities on those of their rival capitalists. The latter employ either a selective integration of the best placed producers or concentrate them in order to be able to place a more telling supply on the market. Commercial contracts are therefore introduced in the cooperative, which undermines the original objectives of the project. The quest for profitability is liable to work against the interests of many farmers. The final result is a purely commercial policy, lacking in a basic ideology of solidarity, causing regrouping by sectors and leaving out of the network all those cooperatives which hinder the achievement of commercial objectives. Thus in taking up the struggle against the capitalist market, there is a risk of creating a cooperative sector which is para-capitalist in form, with no tie to the village economy.

The organization of agricultural work cooperatives varies greatly: they have in common sometimes only one means of production, sometimes all; they have a practice sometimes of shared responsibility, sometimes of co-management or even self-management. A study will be made here of the four more formalized types, which are: agricultural Groups for Common Farming, Agricultural Technical Study Centres, Producers' Groups, and Cooperatives for the Use of Agricultural Machinery. These 13,985 units involve a new conception of work, and a redefinition of the status and functions which society confers on farmers. The initiative of cooperative work arises from the constraints of agrarian individualism, but it aims at transforming it methodically from within, according to its own logic. It adheres to norms and models which combine economy, kinship, and village politics, and are recognized and given specific powers by the state.

The Agricultural Group for Common Farming

This group exemplifies a condensation of the four following elements: 1) economic: holds all means of production in common, shares the power of decision-making, and makes the work collective; 2) kinship: out of a total of 2,755 Groupement agricole d'exploitation en commun (GAEC) in existence in 1972, only 13 percent consist of farmers who have no kinship connection with each other; 3) political: in conferring on each farmer the status of worker and of co-manager, it transforms the significance of work in society; 4) governmental: the state gives it a defined specific function in agricultural politics. This form of cooperative rejects the industrial concentration of labor, and its collectivization into large units, prevents the domination of capital over labor, and combines the social and human advantages of family farming with the economic opportunities of genuine co-management enterprise.

As any organization of men and not of capital, the Group makes common use of the means of production and labor with a view to sharing the benefits. Its interests are communal and not commercial. The work, the marketed produce, consequently the income, retain the same legal and fiscal status as they would for an individual farmer. It is an organization of workers since, legally, its members must work in common. Generally this principle is extended to common management, and any recourse to hired labor is strictly regulated. The number of hired workers cannot exceed the number similarly on family farms in the region.

These cooperatives cultivate 273,237 hectares, which is somewhat less than one percent of the arable land. The average size of each enterprise is 99 hectares, which is five times as much as the average holding in France. Each unit consists, on the average, of three cooperators. Salaried personnel is relatively rare, nonexistent in six cases out of ten, and the use of hired labor is generally decreasing. The Agricultural Groups for Common Farming represent an important concentration of land per worker, but more significant is the number of professionally trained personnel included in their ranks: two out of every three have at least one professionally qualified member, whereas the proportion is only one out of ten for French farmers as a whole. Finally, they show great interest in assuming responsibility in the realm of agricultural organizations, with eight cooperators out of ten taking on outside responsibilities of this kind, as against one out of ten in the case of the other farmers. Factors such as free time, experience in discussion, and familiarity with collective decision-making processes largely account for this interest.

The Workers' Cooperatives are in an unusual economic position
compared to other agricultural arrangements: six out of ten hold more
than 100 hectares. They are in a position to experiment with innovations, due to endless re-orientation of production and frequent holding
of specialized workshops. But their main innovation is in the social
sphere: they transform the family helper or the neighbor,and sometimes the hired worker, into associates on an equal footing, cooperative partners. In two out of three cases, management is common,
notably where equal capital investment or similar educational background exist. In accordance with this, more than one out of every two
cooperatives practices a policy of equal remuneration for its cooperators, regardless of their initial capital contribution. Nevertheless,
co-management with hired labor is still rare; some explain this in
terms of their inability to invest capital as well as their lack of competence. For the same reasons, women are on the whole kept out of
economic jobs and management.

How effective are such achievements in the long run as better
use of capital, growing specialization, more rational organization of
work, the practice of common responsibility, increase of leisure
time, and separation of family and work? There is no doubt that a
new society is in the making when an enterprise is transformed by re-
ducing the use of hired labor, by raising the meaning of solidarity
to the level of collective co-management, and by giving the worker
priority over capital. But these achievements cannot reach their
fullest potential when used only for the benefit of a minority in ex-
ceptional circumstances. In the village they are an economic force
which upsets a great many traditions before they begin to function as
a development factor for the whole community.

Agricultural Technical Study Centers

These are striking in that they are cooperatives of ideas,
economy, and politics which combine differently. The kinship group
and the neighborhood are replaced by mutual trust and understanding,
often resulting from common participation in a youth movement, and
are sustained by the similarity of problems to be solved. As a result,
this form of cooperative is always an inter-village one. The Centers
for Agricultural Technical Study make an essential factor of production commonly available: technical expertise and information.
They consist on the average of about fifteen farmers, and their aim
is to continually reshape their enterprises in a way that will render
them more suited to an industrial economy. The means at their

disposal are threefold: the desire to respond to the daily problems of
members, a system of teamwork in which each member supplies all
available information without concealing from his fellow cooperators,
and financial self-sufficiency, which, in fact, never goes beyond about
50 percent of their requirements.

These idea-cooperatives are characterized above all by a
highly concentrated system of reciprocal information. In principle,
each Center produces a report of its meetings which it distributes
among the regional groups and the national federation for the benefit
of all. As a center of studies, it experiments with prototypes of agricultural projects. Meetings, often held monthly, are obligatory, and
absentees are sometimes penalized. The center supplies the village
with proposals and systems of reference but refrains from extension
activities. Its economic strength is a result of the size of the work
units; one out of two centers controls at least 50 hectares. But still
more of its strength comes from the technical knowhow which is
demonstrated by the two following examples: In 1967, the annual production of milk per cow for the whole of France was identical with
that of the Centres d'Etudes Techniques Agricoles (CETA) for 1959;
CETA farmers used twice as much nitrate per hectare as other farmers.

The 691 Centers for Technical Agricultural Studies aim to be
laboratories where farmers are kept informed. The work team is one
of the principal elements: they produce a blueprint which combines
the responsible participation of farmers at all levels of the economy,
with emphasis on professional training and information, an optimistic
goal of mastery of the future, and the creation of small homogeneous
groups of voluntary members. Since these cooperators consider themselves prototypes they are not organically connected with the village.
Nonetheless, they wield an immense influence in their capacity of
model types, even though the state does not concede them any legal
recognition by its agricultural policy. While displaying a type of
initiative that emphasizes economic qualities of agrarian individualism,
the Centers of Technical Agricultural Studies form an inter-village
network from which the individual village benefits.

Producers' Groups

This is not true of the third form of cooperative agriculture,
the Producers' Groups. Originally spontaneous associations of
farmers engaged in identical production these groups were formed
to improve their economic standing on the market; they became by
the 1960 and 1962 laws specially privileged organizations in terms

of the general agricultural policy of the country. They can be defined by their practice of independent planning of production organized by the farmers themselves, affecting the quality and quantity of products, and by their self-discipline in the matter of marketing, which is rationally adjusted to supply and demand. A continual supply of information regarding the planning and implementation of the producers is necessary. Each of them is strictly limited to a circumscribed area of action, as well as to clearly defined sectors of production. Rules are imposed on the cooperators and carried out in statutes, which they obey; the state controls their activities, subsidizes their function, and penalizes any irregularities, eventually eradicating them. The cooperatives must achieve financial solvency within five years. To this end, they levy compulsory registration and subscription fees, assessed according to the value of commercial produce at a level fixed by the general assembly of members. Thus they pay the technicians and replenish the fund for the stabilization of prices. In a sense the farmer gives up the direct control of sales; the group chooses its buyer, fixes prices, and usually also collects the returns. Complete compliance is obligatory; refusal is penalized by exclusion or by indemnities to be paid for causing damages to the group as a whole. The concentration of supply operated by the 963 Producers' Groups reinforces the economic power of the farmers.

Each one of the Producers' Groups has an average of 335 members, though the variations in size are great; one out of three contains less than fifty cooperators and only one out of ten has more than 500. Whether the cooperators feel that they are really taking an active part in the implementation of agricultural policy is another question. Can this kind of feeling in fact arise where planning is so narrowly sectorial, and within a framework that has been superimposed on the village economy?

The Cooperative for the Use of Agricultural Machinery

This fourth type of cooperative agriculture has a form and significance different from any of the others. Strangely enough, it is the only one included in the Law of Cooperatives, and is ranked on a level with the other commercial cooperatives. They number 9,275, six to every 1,000 farms. Their main technical function is harvesting or threshing, followed by fertilization and tilling of the soil. Insofar as it carries on the tradition of the windmill, the wine press, and the communal bakery, this form of cooperative is relatively old. Due to exigencies imposed by the type of work, it is

essentially confined to the village. In any given district one out of two
confines its activities to the Commune; in the whole of France, nearly
one out of every two operates from a town hall.

The Cooperative for the Use of Agricultural Machinery functions
as an institution with a village economic strategy and not simply as a
response to a technical problem; its function is facilitated by ties of
kinship, neighborhood or mutual confidence. The need to increase production, the heightened cost of mechanization for small enterprises,
the excessive financial burden caused by partial use of machinery, and
the reduction in labor, constitute several aspects of this strategy,
which aims at providing the necessary machinery while avoiding the
risks of overmechanization. One indication of its efficiency is to be
found in the relation between the number of members and its annual
financial turnover. In one district the average number of cooperators
per working unit is seventeen, each member contracting work for 410
francs yearly. In other districts, where the average size is twenty
members, the cooperative carries out 66,000 working hours per year.
In the whole of France, 20 percent of combine-threshers and harvesters
and two percent of all tractors are estimated to be employed in cooperatives.

Another outcome of the machinery cooperative, and not one of
the least, is the necessity for common programming of the agricultural work. It promotes social ties among farmers, often based on
earlier forms of mutual aid. It also gives rise to a series of other
forms of cooperative work such as the Groups for Common Farming.
It represents a modern way of getting around the demands of agrarian
individualism. Finally, by means of cooperative use of machines, the
farmer benefits from increased productivity and bigger returns while
giving up his status of individual proprietor. It is true that this organization cannot be termed a true cooperative of the masses. Its members
are much younger than the other farmers, are often professionally
trained, and are more eager to assume outside responsibility; their
farms are also considerably larger than the average.

The cooperative distribution of agricultural mechanization
operates in accordance with the social and economic logic of the
village and brings about a new kind of social development in it. However, it does not always assure optimal equipment of the village,
subject as it often is to the hazards of local empiricism. Only in rare
instances do we find communes where the cooperative machinery is
regarded as a desirable instrument of collective work planning. To
make this possible the cooperative should not be considered primarily
as a simple service activity for individual farms, but would have to
become a productive factor in its own right. Financial aid, when
eventually granted, would have to be devoted to machinery, as an

instrument of a policy involving the complementary and mutual interdependence between diverse cooperatives. In short, the machinery cooperative will have to break with agrarian individualism in order to
think in the style of a "work commune," in the sense of the political
commune. But these are proposals that look to an analysis of the difficult relations that exist between cooperative initiative and agricultural policy.

COOPERATIVE INITIATIVE AND AGRICULTURAL POLICY

The sociology of the relations between the village and the state,
has, up till now, been neglected; though it is an essential chapter in
political sociology, it has been arbitrarily limited to electoral behavior. It affects the correct analysis of relations between cooperative initiative and agricultural policies. It is possible to formulate
the hypothesis that the forms taken by cooperative agricultural initiative in France are to be explained by the fact that the state, ultimately
responsible for economic policy, ignores the village. Symbolic of this
is the fact that the village is absent from the Rural Code (Code rural),
and that the Commune has no institutionalized link with the Ministry
of Agriculture. In effect the state civilly and politically recognizes
individuals, and economically only recognizes agricultural farms.
For a long time the cornerstone of agricultural policy has been the
development of the family farm, and the "orientation agricole" laws
of 1960 and 1962, with their different clauses, have constructed the
theory of this policy.

It is in the village that the need and drive for regrouping is
mainly felt. The state is constantly transforming the village into
administrative units, with the result that the neighborhood links have
to be remodelled for the work if agrarian individualism is to be
avoided. Moreover, agricultural policies, oriented as they are to
promoting family farming, consist of elements juxtaposed in time—a
fact which the farmers themselves fail to realize. Farmers have the
sole responsibility for initiating cooperative work: such as initiative
is tolerated, codified and subsidized by public policy wherever ex-
pedient without any understanding of what it signifies, in the Weberian
sense at least. Private initiative and cooperative initiative are thus
treated unequally, the latter being merely tolerated, while the former
is publicly desired since it complies with predominant patterns.

The forms of cooperative agrarian work, three of which enjoy
legal status, have no organic relationship as a result of a pre-
established political plan. Each is autonomous, institutionally in

opposition to the others, refraining from connections with the commercialized cooperatives. The strength of village creativity, as well as its weakness in overall efficiency, is derived from the fact that its initiative is not primarily political. Thus the farmers themselves individually compensate for the defects of these parallel organizations, which are mutually ignorant of each other's existence. That many of them participate in two, three, or even four forms of cooperatives, is indicative of the fact that they are more complementary than conflicting.

The last characteristic of agricultural policies is their tendency to centralization. Ignoring history, they fight against the individual character of each village and do not collaborate with it in the elaboration of projects that concern it. They misunderstand cooperative initiative, even though it is reinforced by local kinship or neighborhood ties and confidence which are transformed into an institution by common difficulties. The policies are at the same time individualistic, narrowly economic, over-sectoral, and fractional. Undoubtedly they encounter one important difficulty in that agrarian cooperative enterprise is endowed with a strong degree of sociability, being influenced by considerations such as affinities, friendship, common projects, or kinship relations, which exclude those with no such bonds. Policy, however, is theoretically egalitarian, asserting equal rights for all, and ignoring none. Although not the product of a political initiative, the village could become the proponent of an economic policy in which all could sign as co-authors and which would benefit all, just as in a cooperative.

Thanks to the initiative of the farmers a type of cooperative reconstruction of the village is now taking place. The latter are dispensing with many of their former constraints in order to reorganize in a form which encompasses more space, is economically more diversified, and is socially enriched by the intensity of new relationships. It is still too early to map out these remodelled villages in the absence of statistics; this fact is itself a symptom of the poor coordination between village, cooperative initiative, and policy. Cooperative agriculture should doubtless from the start be considered as the means and objectives of agricultural policies. But for that perhaps we have to wait till history has ridiculed these policies, just as it has refuted the false visions of Proudhon, who in 1851 wrote that "agricultural work is that which least demands, or rather, which most energetically rejects, associated enterprise; peasants have never been known to form any kind of organization for the cultivation of their fields, and never will be."

3

RURAL DEVELOPMENT—
THE CREATION OF A
COLLECTIVE WILL:
SOME FRENCH EXAMPLES
Henri de Farcy

There are numerous activities in collective development in the professional sphere in France. At present 59,000 associations incorporate 1,500,000 French agriculturists and employ some 250,000 paid employees. Volunteers for the presidency and councils of these organizations have to be sought continually.

Readiness for collective action is much rarer when it comes to interests which are outside of the professional sphere. Municipalities (there are approximately 35,000 for 18,000,000 villages) more often represent coalitions of interests than expression of a communal desire for progress. Nevertheless, in recent years there has been a tendency to form organizations that engage in collective action in the non-professional sphere. Unfortunately, these activities have not as yet been subjected to careful analysis because they are dispersed and difficult to identify, they resist classification, and they are extremely diverse in terms of initiatives and initiators. Due to their very nature, they adapt themselves to the economic and social conditions of their environment. They employ original means which are appropriate in their own setting; they cannot be directly imitated.

The following examples, taken from "Espace 90," organ of the "Conféderation Nationale de l'Amenagement Rural," offer a basis for further generalizations.

EXAMPLES OF COLLECTIVE WILL

An Agricultural Cooperative which Directs
its Members to Commercial Activities

The cooperative wine cellar of Rabastens (Tarn) is situated about 30 kilometres from Toulouse. It produces well-matured wine of medium quality. In 1965, it employed about a dozen workers and sold the wine directly to wholesalers.

When two North African repatriates took over the management of the enterprise, they noted that a great many inhabitants of the neighboring towns wanted a wine of known origin. In response to this desire they organized direct deliveries to the home (initially in five to ten litre bottles, later in plastic containers). In 1972, the cellar sold wine in this way to 23,000 subscribers in neighboring towns.

The cooperative is now about to employ 90 persons, mainly local inhabitants. Some (veteran vinegrowers for the most part) perform lighter tasks such as bottling; others undertake office work, deliveries, and more technically advanced jobs. Solicitous and smiling, these young farmers, through their direct contact with customers, have invested their collective enterprise with a favorable image.

This is a good example of collective action in a farming population that has found employment in a field that complements agriculture, without the need for geographical mobility.

The Artisans' and Peasants' Cooperative in Lozère

Two different professions work together in Lozère, an impoverished region in the most rugged part of the French Massif Central. Until recently it had a relatively dense agricultural population. Lately many have left the land for other less onerous and more remunerative occupations. Their neighbors, having expanded somewhat, enjoy slightly better incomes, but they too suffer from periods of under-employment. Rural artisans have seen their markets decrease gradually as a result of the diminishing population.

Recently a group of young farmers and artisans from this area discovered that their "rustic" style was popular with many people, including tourists, and that it offered a new commercial opening. They formed a cooperative in which the artisans work full-time

producing objects for sale as well as taking charge of the running of
the workshops. The farmers work in the off-season. Wages are based
on work done. There are at present 150 members in the cooperative.

Mainly local raw materials—including wood, iron, straw,
wicker, wool, stone, clay, wax, leather, and enamels—are used in
the making of traditional objects such as straw-bottomed chairs,
wrought-iron decorative rails, and pottery, all of which are retailed
in two special shops, one at Mende, the capital of Lozère, and the
other in Paris.

Of special interest in this cooperative activity is the fact that
it draws together in one enterprise people who formerly had only the
traditional buyer-supplier relationship.

Communal Activity

Some years ago a young economist from Montpellier, on becoming mayor of Saint-Mathieu-de-Treviers (534 inhabitants, 25
kilometres from Montpellier), set about establishing a youth and
cultural center. Sports, dances, and certain creative arts, such as
ceramics, were encouraged there. It provided the people with a new
and neutral meeting ground and released certain tensions.

The second phase of communal activity consisted of housing
construction and the introduction of an industrial enterprise supervised by a new industrial plant at Montpellier.

At the present time the total population (more than 1,000) shows
extreme diversification: apart from the traditional farming and non-
farming inhabitants of the village (mainly businessmen) there are
now local industrial workers and workers employed at Montpellier.
Regular meetings are organized to encourage contact. These are
methodically organized by a community worker who is also a teacher
at the University of Montpellier.

In this case collective development started with a desire for
communal cultural activity and moved into the economic and social
fields.

Inter-community Associates

There are certain inter-community associations which make
an effort to express a collective will.

Montrevel-en-Bresse is a district (10,000 inhabitants, 14
communities), which was revived largely due to the efforts of a

country doctor who gained the support of some local people. He knew
how to enlist the help of the communities, without requiring any
financial sacrifice from them: The innovations set in motion by the
new committee were paid from taxes, as were all other district
services. The region has a large enough population to supply personnel for the various activities embarked upon, such as educational
establishments (including a network of secondary education), old age
homes, rest houses, and industrial activities. Great importance is
also given to a recreation area, part of which is designated for water
sports, which should prove an important way of attracting new residents

   In Yonne a regrouping comprising five cantons, 29 communes,
and 29,000 inhabitants is the result of the initiative of the farmers
themselves, who made a joint effort regarding problems with their
land holdings, such as re-parcellation, reorganization, and drainage.
Gradually people of other occupations organized around this nucleus.
The grouping of the communities is conducted by a development committee which is made up of delegates of the communities and of the
trade unions who divide their activities among four committees: agricultural, industrial, artisan, and commercial. The presidents of
these four branches form the directorate. Various centers, easily
accessible to all, are planned, including a college and an industrial
and artisan park, and sports and cultural needs are to be catered for.

WHAT IS THE ORIGIN OF THE COLLECTIVE WILL?

Who were the initiators of this kind of collective development?
Were they able to insure active participation of the population?

   An investigation was made in 1970 in which 1250 communities
participated in a "My Favorite Village" contest which required proof
of achievement in development. First an attempt was made to define
the motivating agents of these innovations. This was not a matter of
rigid classification since the sampling of communities was not entirely representative. Moreover, the interviewed may have designated
as motivating agents the more striking though less efficient personalities at the expense of the more modest, but more efficient ones.

   In spite of these reservations it is interesting to note that municipal bodies were among those most often cited as motivating agents
(about 60 percent). The explanation for this is probably the fact that
it is necessary to conscript a certain amount of public support in
stimulating a cooperative will of the kind that sets in motion these
innovations. Confirmation of this fact generally emerges in the course
of municipal elections. This percentage is higher than that of other

associations (17 percent) or to youth groups (9 percent); and 42 percent of the "motivating agents" are private individuals, three-quarters of whom are local people, the rest outsiders. (The total percentage in replies is higher than 100 percent since sometimes more than one agent was cited.)

We can conclude from these results that any innovation, if it is to proceed from the stage of mere suggestion to that of implementation, has to have the support of persons with effective public backing.

The investigation attempted to verify the rate of public participation. This was done by taking into account the total number of inhabitants and not only those who were accessible. Not everyone is able to take advantage of a swimming pool or a sports arena, to give but one example. With this reservation in mind, it was asserted that these initiatives were followed by participation of the entire population in only 29 percent of the cases. Associations participated in 48 percent of the cases, private individuals in 42 percent, and youth in 37 percent.

It would be interesting to find out what diverse influences—such as travel abroad or militant action—affected the motivating agents themselves.

WHERE IS THE COLLECTIVE WILL APPLICABLE?

I was struck by the number of cases in which the creation of a collective will has commenced with what I term the "new" and the "neutral." "New" realizations are those in which the relationships between individuals or groups are not of a traditional type. "Neutral" activities are those which old oppositions (political, religious, ideological, and social) do not find it necessary to resist.

The following examples illustrate the above.

Festivals

The inhabitants of Haute-Rivoire, a village near Lyon which has seen many economic and social innovations, began a joint celebration of Saint Jean in torchlight processions with the opening of a traditional museum in the village clocktower, and with the creation of an organization interested in hunting horns.

In another village, Laurede (Gard), parties for campers were organized; the farmers sold grilled meat in the market square and geese and ducks were cooked free of charge. On Sundays the organizers gave a free liter of wine and a bouquet of flowers

Communal activities, such as a dancehall and a swimming pool, set up in 1935 by the Vandre (Charentes) community, later facilitated the promotion of lotteries and the construction of factories.

Recreation and Sport

In many cases groups of young people agreed to volunteer for work with the object of contributing to the cost of sports equipment. In the village of Pomillon (Landes), 52 youngsters contributed the equivalent of 1,800 to 2,000 working days in a period of three years, by which 50,000 francs out of a total cost of 200,000 were earned. Older people (such as businessmen, quarrymen, and foresters) subscribed 30,000 francs in goods as gifts. As a result, the community spent no more than 120,000 francs.

Culture

The same sort of enthusiasm was exhibited in the restoration of an old château (château of Goute-las, Marcoux-en-Forez, Loire) donated by a farmer to serve as a cultural center; thirty thousand working hours were contributed by peasants, engineers, and workers from the neighboring town.

The Château of Harcourt, in Normandy, was likewise renovated through the good services of a local organization of young farmers.

Every kind of activity which promotes cultural integration at the local level can be classified with the above. For example, all kinds of folkloristic and other planned cultural activities, historically and traditionally oriented which have as their object the revival of a communal raison d'être, stemming from a consciousness of a common past.

Beauty

Six million French homes, half of the total, have gardens and cultivate them in a spirit of strong but friendly competition. This is reflected in contests for the most decoratively planted railway station, the most attractive customs houses, and so on. Village flower shows too have often proved the springboard for more far-reaching operations.

Such was the case in Pas-de-Calais, a village where the farmers moved by means of mechanical equipment 90 tons of debris which had been cluttering up the sidewalks. They then set fire to thistles, pruned trees and hedges, and deposited 300 tons of rubble in order to reduce the cost of laying a country road while their children painted the curbstones white for two kilometers.

Informal Meetings

These various activities are often augmented by informal meetings organized among the inhabitants, in which outsiders are occasionally invited to take part. Thus, for example, crews clearing away rubble organize parties in the evenings, leading to lively and easy contact among young people.

It is interesting to note that in numerous cases, such modest, unremunerative activities have paved the way for much more complex operations leading to economic and social development.

CONCLUSION

It appears that the innovators responsible for these activities have rediscovered, quite by instinct, certain fundamentals of the laws of integrated development. They have acted as "animators," in the sense that they help people to initiate communal action by means which had not previously been fully utilized.

Can these types of activity not be linked to what some economists call "the policy of economic growth"? While "scale economies" seek the optimal size for each element of a structure, "growth economies" attempt to foster the dormant and badly used elements. This theory has obvious application to the utilization of unexploited natural resources. Our "animators" have, to date, succeeded in focusing attention on the following:

- voluntary development of personal ability
- dedication of leisure time to public ends
- alertness in anticipation of mistakes or circumstances likely to be of importance in the future
- personal concern for the problems of others
- use of personal relations in the general interest
- development of ability to make decisions and put them into immediate effect

Instead of being critical of others, these "animators" have turned their energies to creating new sources of strength. They have overcome obstacles in two ways: by proposing activities which are at the same time new and neutral, thus eliminating factors which might have prevented individuals or groups from collaborating on a common project; and by their awareness of the fear of being "used" by rivals who would turn the fruits of their labors to their own commercial or political profit, the fear of being recruited for activities of an ideological nature, and the fear of being drawn into unpopular activities.

After working in this type of activity with people from various backgrounds, everyone discards prejudices that arise from mutual ignorance; we learn to compromise and to work together at the economic or political level, without betraying our own basic values.

In addition, the diversity of activities provide the varied categories of participants with the motivation most suited to their social status, their culture, their age, and the extent of their awareness of the need for such things as collective action.

The methods of overcoming obstacles and the diversity of activities do not solve all problems at one time, but make a gradual solution possible.

No general strategy of development is to be implied from these remarks. Completely different factors which are beyond the control of rural communities are decisive in that. But there are certain measures which rural communities can immediately put into practice. The examples cited prove that immediate and effective action can be taken.

4

A DEFINITION OF THE
RURAL COOPERATIVE COMMUNITY
IN DEVELOPING COUNTRIES
Yair Levi

The aim of this paper is to discuss the concept of the rural cooperative community in developing countries and to suggest a minimum definition of it as a possible tool of rural progress. Our approach to the topic will thus be both of a descriptive and normative character.

THE PROBLEM

Till now two major models of cooperative organization seem to have emerged in the rural areas of developing countries: that of the common service cooperatives and that based on collectivistic arrangements. Experience seems to indicate that on the whole the first has made little contribution to change whereas the latter has been often resisted by the local population.

In the course of the following discussion it will be suggested that a village organization overcoming the limitations of service cooperatives and avoiding extreme measures of collectivization can provide an intermediate model for development. Traditional values such as solidarity and the search for security can co-exist, under proper guidance, with such modern values as investment-oriented action, provided the system is flexible enough as to the degree and the tempo of cooperative integration to be obtained.

Discussion will be based on the following premises:

1. The association of the notion of community to that of the village as a clustered geographical unit

29

2. The assumption that the concept of rural cooperative community would be justified only by the extension of activities beyond
the commercial domain of agricultural services

3. The assumption that a maximum of cooperative integration
does not always imply an optimum of development, so that the concept
of rural cooperative community does not necessarily require a socialization of the means of production or a collective system in labor and/or
in the way of living. Also it will be assumed that the affiliation of the
total population of a given village to the common organization is not to
be considered as an indispensable element for the minimum definition
required.

Point one aims at delimiting the physical precondition for a
rural cooperative community. Points two and three aim at defining
the degree of cooperative integration within the village in terms of
activities and membership. The combination of all these elements
will allow for a definition of a minimum of integration that would
justify the attribute of rural cooperative community. Such a definition may later permit the construction of an ascending ladder of degrees
of integration in cooperation, ranging from the suggested minimum
model up to fully integrated rural communities (such as the Israeli
Kibbutz or some of the contemporary Japanese communes).

We shall first confine ourselves to the physical-institutional
preconditions for a rural cooperative community.

PHYSICAL-INSTITUTIONAL ASPECTS

The Village as a Clustered Geographical Unit

A situation of dispersed rural population is ill-suited to the
adoption of policies which aim at the improvement of conditions of life
in rural areas. Economic as well as social diseconomies are likely
to occur in attempts to direct promotion measures and extension
facilities towards dispersed family units. The necessity arises, therefore, for rural planners to overcome the drawbacks arising from the
phenomenon of "dispersed rural population," for which a definition has
been proposed recently by Marshall Wolfe.[1] Despite the dissimilarity
of situations existing in rural areas in different countries, the clustering
of dispersed rural population is increasingly considered a vital objective in order to enable the implementation of community development
policies and the rationalization of production. These efforts lead

planners to consider the concept of "rural community" as linked with
that of the village. "The village incorporates physically the life of the
community and the community is the basic level of action in the rural
development process. "[2]

Within this framework it is possible to avoid duplication of costs
and inefficiencies involved in the provision of services to scattered
farming units. "The rural community or village may be composed of
a group of families whose houses are located in the same area and
who receive their daily essential services from a communal center
within the village. "[3] As for the rationalization of production, this
aim "requires an optimal concentration of built-up zones, preserving
adequate distances to the fields. "[4]

Obviously enough, village planning has to be adapted to local
conditions and no unique solution can be found for different regions.
Techniques for the physical design of villages can be rationally applied in land settlement projects, especially when linked with comprehensive regional planning. Advocating a policy of cooperative promotion
of agricultural production especially in developing countries, Schiller[5]
has made the point that village settlements offer many advantages for
the adoption of these measures as compared with settlements with
isolated farmsteads, owing to the possibility of setting up common installations servicing all the producers in the community. On the other
hand, in old established communities, even those presenting characteristics of clustered settlements, village planning necessarily meets
with a number of major obstacles deriving from traditional structures.
In a general way it can be assumed that cooperative action among
farmers, both in old established, and in newly created villages can be
facilitated by a clustered physical layout of the village, and by appropriate field arrangements.

Uniformity of Economic Status

Striking inequalities in the disposal of the main means of production, especially land, among farmers of the same village, not only
constitute economic and social features incompatible with the essence
of cooperation, but in the long run they can only further weaken the
village structure. The operator of a large farm who employs hired
labor and is attached to the land only for its economic rentability is
not likely to contribute much to his village conceived as a cooperative
community. On the other hand, the owner of a plot which is too small
to be economic and who must struggle for his very existence, will
hardly constitute a favorable element to the creation of a sound cohesive

group. Both types of farmers are supposed to be potential candidates
for rural exodus. In some cases, the desire to preserve the homogeneous composition of the group may dictate the necessity to "violate" the
principle of "open door" and to refuse the admittance to the cooperative
of wealthy landowners who may impair the social cohesion of the
society. [6]

The problem of landless peasants exists alongside the reforms
to be implemented within the framework of existing villages. Both for
new and already existing villages, an equitable distribution of means
of production, especially land, among associated producers should be
considered as a necessary, though not sufficient, condition for initiating
an effective cooperative system. The experience of the Israeli moshav
has demonstrated the importance of an egalitarian starting point for
settlers towards a harmonious evolution of the settlements. This experience has shown that inequalities emerging in time within the village may weaken the very structure of the whole community. As will
be shown further on, the ability to avoiding widening of gaps is a major
yardstick of cooperative viability.

The implementation of land reform and its adaptation to conditions prevailing in various environments, constitute a complex question
not within the scope of this paper. As a general remark, it has to be
stressed that providing associated farmers with maximum equal opportunities to improve their situation does not only imply the formal
application of a system of land distribution, but also aims at creating
a new feeling of security among the beneficiaries. Structural changes,
conceived in this sense, aim at creating a social framework capable
of protecting the rural population against the dangers of instability
and insecurity menacing it. A village of a homogeneous character can
better secure the success of reforms if these can be reinforced by cooperative action. Singh has stressed this point: "Land reform will be
a creating force in the development of the rural economy if it is conceived as a vital element in the building-up of cooperative village communities. In so far as it makes for a more homogeneous village
society, land reform should, therefore, facilitate the development of
cooperation in farming as well as other activities."[7]

COOPERATION WITHIN THE VILLAGE

Integration by Activities

Having presented the structural context which would offer a
favorable basis for a cooperative organization within the village, a
degree of integration by activities has to be delimited extending

beyond the sphere of economic services while still fitting to the definition of rural cooperative community for which we are searching. Common action among farmers in the provision of essential services, such as credit, marketing, and supply, and operation within a clustered and homogeneous settlement as described above, can benefit from conditions which differ considerably from those prevailing in most cooperative societies in the rural areas of developing countries. Extending cooperation beyond those services to additional domains, such as supervised credit for production, crop planning, use of machines, and irrigation, would not suceed without previous physical-institutional arrangements within the village. Schiller[8] has discussed in detail the conception of cooperative promotion of agricultural production and described the ways of its implementation in countries at different stages of development. He considers cooperative promotion of agricultural production—a form of organization based on cooperative decision-making in some farming operations still preserving the individual use of land—as an effective means enabling rural cooperatives to overcome limitations inherent in the usual service cooperatives with a view to increasing agricultural yields and improving production methods.

But if a rural community has to care for the welfare and livelihood of its members, cooperation will have to cover non-economic domains as well. Provision of basic local services such as a village school, a cultural center, and sanitary, health, and other community facilities, should be considered as inseparable from a community-oriented structure. As it develops the village organization may assume municipal tasks as well. The underlying idea is that under favorable conditions the village cooperative should become the leading factor in running the village. This point will be discussed in more detail below.

One major issue for investigation may be to assess the extent to which the provision of services can be secured in a viable way by a single village committee of a multi-functional character. It can be assumed that a multi-functional management body operating at the village level can allow for social and economic economies and for a better use of scarce qualified personnel.

To sum up the foregoing, a rural cooperative community is characterized by the presence of cooperation in at least the three following domains: economic services, production planning, and social services and/or community facilities. In this way, without weakening the family as a basic social and economic unit, members of the cooperative organization can actively take part in running the affairs of the village. Such a pattern of cooperative integration should be considered as a minimum for a community oriented village structure to enable it to overcome some limitations inherent in

service societies and to provide at the same time a basis for the
transfer of additional functions from the individual to the collective
domain.

Integration by Membership

A pragmatic approach must also be adopted with regard to integration by membership. Whereas radical changes can be obtained
within a relatively short time in cases of resettlement projects,
patient work involving education, training, and demonstration may be
needed when reforms are carried out in the framework of old established communities. A few practical examples may help illustrate
some aspects of the issue.

The experience of Indian cooperative farming is the first case
in point. In the case of both the joint farming societies and in those of
the collective farming type, planners aimed at extending cooperation
beyond the scope covered by conventional service societies. It appears
however that the implementation of reforms not only lags behind plans,
but has not yet been fulfilled in most cases, at the level of the whole
village. Cooperative organization includes a relatively small percentage of farmers from the same village or is composed of groups belonging to different locations. Social stratification and socio-economic
inequalities have a negative effect on the size of cooperative societies.
The prominent role that castes play in rural India has led some authors
to question the sociological reality of the Indian village and to ask
whether the caste, and not the village, should be the proper unit of
study. [9] In his criticism of Indian cooperative farming societies,
Bergmann[10] has pointed out that lack of homogeneity within many of
the operating farming societies prevents them from exercising a
favorable influence on the whole village.

If we consider the second example, the Israeli moshav, as a
case of integrated cooperative settlement, we can observe a complete
identification of the cooperative organization and the village as a
municipal body. Although based on individual farming, the moshav
cannot be considered a conventional village of small holders since it
presents the features of a self-governing community whose cooperative regulations affect all its inhabitants in most spheres of their
lives.

The two examples cited originated and developed under
completely different circumstances. Viewed outside their specific
environment and evaluated in light of the objectives of our analysis,

we can hardly see either of them as satisfactory for the minimum definition we are seeking: the Indian formula of cooperative farming because of its weak impact on the whole village, and the moshav because of the complete overlapping of the cooperative organization and the village as a municipal unit.

Another type of village in Israel provides a cooperative formula which may offer some elements to our definition. In this type, the adherence of the majority of the farmers to the local cooperative is considered a sufficient criterion for the registration of the village as a cooperative one. Situated between the moshav and a village of private farmers, this type of settlement has developed a cooperative system of common services, mutual assistance, and joint production in some branches. The most important feature distinguishing these cooperative villages from the cooperative settlements—Kibbutz, Moshav Shitufi and Moshav Ovdim—is that there is no legal identification of cooperative and municipal functions in the former. The cooperative village contributes to the diversification of village organization in Israel.

Guernier[11] has devoted much thought to the issue of rural cooperative communities in the developing countries. In his opinion the village, as the driving force in a comprehensive rural development, "...should become on its own efforts a cooperative nucleus of development based upon the sole management of the inhabitants." The establishment of cooperative communities should be carried out so as to take into account the specific conditions of each region. A general procedure suggested reads as follows: "A village can become a village community where four-fifths of the family heads decide to do so and to adopt the necessary statutes."

In a similar vein, surveying instances of cooperative villages in African countries Pickett[12] has made the point that these villages deserve the attribute "cooperative" only insofar as the cooperatives become the leading institutions in village life, by means of meeting most of the needs of the majority of the villagers.

Under completely different circumstances, the criterion of the "majority of the adult inhabitants" of a village is considered as a sufficient element for its definition as a cooperative community.

THE COOPERATIVE VILLAGE AS AN AGENT OF CHANGE

A village cooperative community is much more than a mere agglomeration of family units or the aggregate efforts of the producers who live in its boundaries. The building up of an integrated community and of such values as mutual help, responsibility, and solidarity, does not depend on the formal application of cooperative formulas although they may be adapted to local requirements with the utmost care. The cooperative village should not be considered solely as a means of increasing agricultural production. The cooperative village can contribute to the strengthening of rural areas, in their position regarding the urban centers, through radical changes in the way of life of the rural population.

In such a perspective, valid standards of evaluation are:

1. extent to which the cooperative group provides an efficient system of communication from the top down and from the bottom up (both at the local primary level and between the latter and the regional and national levels)
2. extent to which both the net returns and the standard and quality of life of associated members are bettered
3. ability to provide savings and community-oriented investments
4. ability to generate maximum consensus within, together with openness outwards
5. ability to promote local leadership and sufficient overall involvement in village management
6. ability to insure organized action which would prevent, as much as possible, the widening of existing gaps and/or the creation of new ones.

According to recent findings of the cross-national research conducted by the United Nations Research Institute for Social Development,[13] cooperatives in rural developing areas have on the whole failed to generate change. Most of the aforementioned criteria have not been met.

In many developing countries the village unit is often far from presenting a homogeneous and cohesive group. Particularism of clans, social stratification, and inequalities of wealth, power, and status which mark so many agrarian societies in newly developing countries constitute serious obstacles to the engineering of a consensus towards development and the upbuilding of self-managed organizations. Possibilities for building homogeneous groups are greater in new settlement projects, but even there previous habits and traditional behavior must be seriously considered. In view of the above-mentioned constraints and clashes between modernization needs and traditional values, the process of institution-building at the village level is inevitably a slow and often painful one. Chances

of success depend mainly on the extent to which actions conducive
to change are based on "felt needs" which have to be carefully considered in order to insure that they are actually those of the less
privileged groups within a given community, and not restricted to
economic aspects only. Furthermore, the concept of "felt needs" has
to be made operational in light of considerations of broader spatial
dimensions, which means that village development has to be part of
the development of the surrounding region. [14] Once such an approach
is broadly accepted it becomes clear that a straight policy aiming at
creating "ready-made" cooperatives would be counter productive. A
cooperative set up, if it has to be understood as a self-managed group
based on commonly agreed aims and—as much as possible—on homogeneity of interests and composition, has to be the result of carefully
planned cooperative arrangements, according to levels and types of
development.

THE MINIMUM DEFINITION SUMMARIZED

The Criteria

From the foregoing discussion three major factors emerge as
criteria for a minimum definition of a rural cooperative community:

1. Concentratration, at the village level, of habitations, which
   preserves adequate distances to the cultivated plots, allowing
   for rationalization of production and provision of community
   facilities;
2. A multi-functional cooperative set up to extend its activities
   beyond the economic domain;
3. A cooperative membership of the majority of the active
   population within the village.

These factors delimit the physical-geographical aspects of the
organizational setting and describe the scope and intensity of cooperation.
The issue of uniformity of economic status has been mentioned
as a precondition for the building up of a viable cooperative community.
Whereas equality in the allocation of basic means of production (such
as land, water, and credit) can be achieved in new settlement projects,
the problem is much more complicated in settled areas. Of even
greater complexity is the issue of social and ethnic homogeneity. The
Israeli experience has shown that settling of homogeneous ethnic
groups in each new moshav settlement facilitates the process of their
transformation into a cooperative community. The most stable settle-

ments are those in which traditional ties have been preserved and in which the settlers have been united from the start by common origin. On the other hand, the breaking up of family clans and the settlement of families of different origin in the same settlement leads to ceaseless frictions and factionalism which endanger the stability of the communities.[15]

Commentators on cooperative experience in other areas have made the point that under certain circumstances a degree of social heterogeneity can be favorable to cooperative success.[16]

The degree of internal cohesion within a given village has been previously mentioned as a criterion for community orientation. Here we have a criterion which, difficult both to identify and to quantify, cannot be included in our minimum definition. The ability to generate maximum internal consensus for major decisions, especially in cases of distress and emergency, should be considered a most valid yardstick of the efficiency and maturity of any self-managed organization, regardless of its degree of cooperative integration.

A Schematic Presentation

The suggested minimum definition is based upon a qualitative combination of factors. These are taken from the domain of services, partly from that of production (more precisely from what Schiller has termed "cooperative promotion of agricultural production"[17]) and from the domain of more integral forms of cooperation. As already emphasized, the inclusion of social services and/or community facilities in the minimum definition confers to it the community dimension required.

What place should the suggested definition have in a classification of cooperative factors of integration? Several authors have built classifications, starting from service cooperatives as the loosest patterns of integration and ending with the Israeli Kibbutz or other forms of communal organizations. Among these classifications we can mention those of Desroche[18], Schiller[19] and Bergmann[20]. Though built along an ascending line of integration, these classifications lack any reference to the integration by membership which interests us.

Table I aims at a two-dimensional presentation of various elements of integration in rural cooperatives. The membership scale is divided into three levels: low, a membership of less than 50 percent of the total active adult population of a given village; medium, a membership of more than 50 percent; and high, the total active adult population of the village. The activity scale lists most factors of

integration in cooperation as included in existing literature. Due to its
importance for the understanding of village organization in Israel and
to the eventual interest it may have in other countries, identification
of municipal and cooperative functions has been included as a factor
of integration in the "community" dimension.

Three cooperative dimensions have been used to mark three
domains of activities: servicing, production, and community. Varying
degrees of cooperation in these domains give various combinations in
integration, in terms of both activities and membership, within a
given rural locality.

Taking Table 4.1 as a term of reference we shall present some
of the cooperative organizational patterns mentioned in this paper and
show their respective degree of cooperative integration along the two
dimensions. From the empirical field six cases will be considered: a
service society, an Indian cooperative farming society of the collective
type, a cooperative village in Israel, a Moshav Ovdim, a Moshav
Shitufi, and a Kibbutz.

Two theoretical patterns will be considered: a society patterned
after the model of "cooperative promotion of agricultural production"
as suggested by Schiller, and our suggested minimum model of a rural
cooperative community.

The various patterns are shown in Table 4.2.

For the purpose of comparison, the service cooperative society
(no. 1) has been considered as extending its activities to the totality
of the population within the village. The example of an Indian cooperative farming society of the collective type (no. 3) has been considered
as covering social activities as well.

The suggested minimum model (no. 4) is ranked lower than no. 1
in terms of integration by membership, and lower than no. 3 as regards
integration by activities. However no. 4 compensates for the absence
of coverage of the total population by a more even distribution of activities than no. 1, mainly by affecting the community area. On the other
hand no. 4 compensates for the absence of integration in such domains
as common production and a collective land tenure system (which are
not essential elements in our community based definition), by a wider
geographical coverage than no. 3, so as to include the majority of the
village population. The model of cooperative promotion of agricultural
production, no. 2, shares with no. 4 a pragmatic approach to integration in farming activities as well as the coverage of the majority of
the village population, yet it lacks the community dimension.

This table finally shows that pattern no. 4 falls behind the Israeli
moshav, the lowest pattern in the category of cooperative settlements
to which also the Moshav Shitufi and the Kibbutz belong. This is so because we consider that some of the basic tenets common to all settlements of this category (such as collective ownership of land and the

TABLE 4.1

A Two-Dimensional Presentation of Possibilities of Integration in Rural Cooperatives

	The Membership Scale		
Domain and Factor of Integration	Low <50 percent	Medium >50 percent	High Σ
1.1 Marketing of agriculture produce			
1.2 Credit and supply of agricultural inputs			
1.3 Processing, transportation, insurance, and related services to farmers			
2.1 Use of machines and irrigation			
2.2 Animal husbandry			
2.3 Production planning and supervised credit			
2.4 Production in farm activities			
2.5 Production in non-farm activities			
2.6 Land ownership			
3.1 Social services and/or community facilities			
3.2 Municipal functions (as fulfilled by village cooperative)			
3.3 Purchase of food and home supplies			
3.4 Consumption			
3.5 Care of children			
3.6 Living quarters of youth and adults			

Servicing Service Co-operatives

Production Production Cooperatives

Community Integral Cooperatives

The Activities Scale

TABLE 4.2

Patterns of Integration in Various Types of Rural Cooperative Organizations

Factor and domain of integration[a] Type of Organization	1 Service cooperative society	2 Cooperative promotion of agricultural production	3 Indian Cooperative farming (collective)	Rural Cooperative Communities				
				4 Suggested minimum model	5 Cooperative village-Israel	6 Moshav Ovdim	7 Moshav Shitufi	8 Kibbutz
Servicing								
1.1	C[b]	C	C	C	C	C	C	C
1.2	C	C	C	C	C	C	C	C
1.3	C	C	C	C	C	C	C	C
Production								
2.1		C	C	C	C[c]	C[c]	C	C
2.2		C	C				C	C
2.3		C	C	C	C	C[c]	C	C
2.4			C			C[c]	C	C
2.5								C
2.6			C			C	C	C
Community								
3.1			C	C	C	C	C	C
3.2						C	C	C
3.3						C	C	C
3.4								C
3.5								C
3.6								C[c]
Place on membership scale[a]	High	Medium	Low	Medium	Medium	High	High	High

[a]See Table 4.1
[b]Cooperative or collective
[c]Individual

Source: Compiled by the authors.

41

TABLE 4 3

A Combined Membership Activities
Typology of Patterns of Cooperative Integration

		Membership Scale*		
		Low	Medium	High
	Low	partial few 1	majority few 2	total few 3
Activities Scale	Medium	partial many 4	majority many 6	total many 7
	High	partial maximum 5	majority maximum 8	total maximum 9

*1 = Service society with limited membership;
6 = Suggested minimum model;
9 = Total village community (for example, the Kibbutz).
Source: Compiled by the author.

identification of municipal and cooperative functions) are not necessary
elements in a minimum definition of a rural cooperative community.
It ensues that broadly speaking no. 4 is equivalent to no. 5 (the cooperative village).

The two scales of Table 4.2 can be combined in a simplified presentation according to three levels of integration. Low, medium, and
high can be related respectively to partial, majority, and total (the
membership scale) and to few, many, and maximum (the activities
scale). In such a way, a typology of combinations can be obtained in
which the intermediate location of the minimum model suggested becomes apparent.

CONCLUDING REMARKS

The main idea behind this paper is to show that the concept of the cooperative village should be rethought so as to allow for a combination of community-wide action within a minimum framework of integration at the village level. The content of the preceding pages should be considered as a preliminary attempt to stimulate discussion on the topic. Refinement of conceptual approaches and relevant data collection may enable us to ascertain the extent to which a minimum definition of the rural cooperative community can provide a viable point of reference for a better knowledge of the issue.

Such a survey should permit identification of empirical cases, which may either not meet requirements for a minimum definition, meet them, or surpass them. Once data are collected and arranged into a sort of typology of existing structures, research can be conducted for the purpose of obtaining more knowledge about the feasibility and viability of various integrated cooperative organizations at the village level.

Empirical evidence shows in most cases combinations of the individual and the collective in domains of integration, which hardly fit any theoretical minimum definition. The value of a theoretical construction is that it provides a term of reference with some directions of a normative character. For instance, one may find cooperative systems at the initial stages of settlement based on a total membership of the farming population within the village in a few domains of activity, such as credit and marketing. In our opinion this does not challenge the rationale underlying the proposed definition. In fact it can be assumed that a community based village cooperative does not emerge until common action encompasses social functions as well.

The idea of the integrated village community has been a challenge in different epochs and in widely differing cultural contexts, either as a means of organization and social reform, or more recently, as a tool of overall rural development.

From the early nineteenth century utopias to contemporary rural communes, from the Japanese Yamaghishi to the Indian Sarvodaya movement, and from the Tanzanian Ujamaa to the Israeli-modelled villages in various developing countries, a wide range of ideological approaches and operational devices can be observed in which cooperative practices under informal or formal status play a major role.

As in the past, idealization of the cooperative village will presumably continue in the years to come, due to the possibility it offers

to planners and policy-makers in differing socio-political systems to
add an element of prestige to local aspirations of rural development.

Those countries eager to launch attractive programs of "villagi-
zation" should be aware of the possibilities of pragmatic approaches.
It is suggested that even targets of village development of relatively
limited scope such as the one presented in this paper should be considered as long-term goals, rather than the object of massive program
expected to yield quick results.

NOTES

1. "Although no common denominator for dispersion has been
established the definition proposed by Marshall Wolfe in his typology
of rural settlements, can be adopted to visualize the scope of this
phenomenon. According to this definition, the limit for a dispersed
pattern of settlement is the maximum of twenty people." Marshall
Wolfe, quoted in Report of the Interregional Seminar on Rural Housing
and Community Facilities, Maracay, Venezuela, April 2-19, 1967
(New York: United Nations, 1968): 103.

2. Ibid., p. 106.

3. Ibid., p. 112.

4. Ibid., p. 106.

5. O. Schiller, Cooperation and Integration in Agricultural
Production (Bombay: Asia Publishing House, 1969), p. 73.

6. T. Bergmann, Funktionen und Wirkungsgrenzen von
Produktions-genossenschaften in Entwicklungsländern. (Frankfurt:
Europäische Verlagsanstalt, 1967), p. 36.

7. T.C. Singh, "The Cooperative Village," The Economic Week
Annual (New Delhi, January, 1958).

8. O. Schiller, Cooperation and Integration, op. cit., pp. 48-92.

9. A. Beteille, "Ideas and Interests: Some Conceptual Problems
in Study of Social Stratification in Rural India," International Social
Science Journal, 21, no. 2 (1969): 217-34.

10. T. Bergmann, Funktionen und Wirkungsgrenzen, op. cit.,
p. 193.

11. M. Guernier, La dernière chance du Tiers Monde (Paris:
R. Laffont, 1966), pp. 200-06.

12. E. Pickett, "Cooperative Villages in African Countries,"
Cooperative Information, I.L O., No. 1, 1970: pp. 55-66.

13. United Nations Research Institute for Social Development
(UNRISD), Rural Cooperatives as Agents of Change in Developing
Areas, six vol. (Geneva, 1970-72).

14. For a detailed discussion of the potentials and limitations of cooperatives within a pluralistic institutional setting at the regional level, see Y. Levi, "Institution Building through Self-Help in Rural Developing Areas: an Integrated Approach," International Review of Community Development, no. 31-32 (Summer 1974): 261-93.

15. See Y. Landau and A. Rokach, "Rural Development in Israel," in: Rural Development in a Changing World eds. R. Weitz and Y. Landau (Cambridge, Mass.: M.I.T. Press, 1971), p. 486-500.

16. T.F. Carroll, "Peasant Cooperation in Latin America," In A Review of Rural Cooperation in Developing Areas: Rural Institutions and Planned Change (Geneva: United Nations Research Institute for Social Development, 1969), p. 74.

17. Schiller, op. cit., pp. 48-63.

18. M. Desroche, Coopération et Développement. Mouvements Coopératifs Stratégie du Développement. (Paris: Presses Universitaires de France, 1964).

19. Schiller, op. cit., p. 10.

20. Bergmann, "Factors Influencing Optimum Size and Decision Making on Cooperative Farms," Sociologia Ruralis, 9, no. 2 (1969): 114-33.

5

COOPERATION AND
DIFFERENTIAL PRICES
IN RURAL REGIONS
Yves Le Balle

As an institution, the cooperative cannot be separated from the socio-economic aims it seeks to achieve; it is a tool serving a specific development project in which solidarity and education are assigned important roles. It seeks to substitute advancement based on mutual aid, in the Kropotkin sense, for the Darwinian "progress by elimination."[1] Cooperative success is not measured solely or even chiefly by the value added to things, but by its ability to add value to people who take part in collective, creative work.

However, the situation of an agricultural cooperative functioning within a capitalist market economy is more complicated. The cooperative has the double function of producing commodities and of dispensing collective services. It is thus bound by a double logic: it must survive and grow in an environment which it has not chosen, and must therefore remain 'competitive,' and it is supposed to serve the collective advantage of the producers who are its members and of the rural region as a whole.

Those two aims are not always compatible. The need to survive and grow may result in a conflict with the requirements of solidary development. In such a situation the logic of the capitalist system may become so overpowering that the cooperative resorts to practices which discriminate between its members, from the introduction of differential prices* to a policy of more or less systematic elimination of producers who are unfavorably located, in arrears, or too small.

---

*Prices are differential whenever the same product is paid for, or the same service is charged, at different prices to different members of the same cooperative.

The actual behavior of the cooperatives thus often seems quite at odds with the original project. Such practices, which have recently become more frequent, have produced tensions and conflicts among the member producers or with the agricultural trade unions in several regions. This suggests two lines of inquiry. First, at what point will a differential price policy result in tensions that seriously prejudice the functioning of the institution? This is the question of how a decision of this kind will be accepted, and is therefore of an entirely pragmatic order. Second, to what extent do decisions run counter to the solidarity principle of the cooperative development project? This is a question of a more fundamental nature, bearing upon cooperative ideology.

ANALYSIS OF FACTS

We were able to establish first of all that discriminatory practices, particularly differential prices, were in the majority of cases introduced first by capitalistic enterprises—the cooperatives followed suit after a certain interval of time.

Subsequently, it became evident to us that there is no discontinuity or absolute separation between the application of differential prices by a cooperative and its elimination of certain categories of members: elimination is different only in degree, being a border case of discrimination to which the cooperative resorts when its economic situation deteriorates and the management admits that it is unable to solve its problems in any other way.

Finally, observation of the facts suggests that price differentiation is of three types, according to whether the difference is made in terms of situation benefits, capacity for progress, or production volume.

DIFFERENTIATION IN TERMS OF SITUATION BENEFITS

Let us consider a purchasing cooperative which receives fertilizers by rail and distributes it by truck to all the farmers of the region, charging the same price for all. In doing so, it calculates its price per sack so as to include the average cost of transport, and thus allows the most remote farms to benefit from an implied cost equalization. This solution is generally regarded as equitable by the cooperative membership.

Now suppose there is a merchant who decides to sell fertilizers only to the producers nearest to the railway, but at a lower price than that of the cooperative. He can afford to do so, because his transport costs are lower, and consequently he allows the most advantageously located farmers to enjoy a benefit of situation. In that case, the co-operative is forced to adjust its prices to those of the merchant in the nearer zone, while raising the price paid by the more remote producers. Failing this, it may have to abandon the most profitable zones to private commerce and serve only the more remote enterprises without being able to avoid raising its prices; in fact, the price increase may have to be even larger.

Unless there is a collective reaction by the producers of the entire region which succeeds in forcing the merchant and the farmers nearest to the railway—and possibly even the management of the cooperative—to conform to the former practice, the cooperative alone is incapable of defending its mutual development project, which does not follow the rules of the game of the capitalist market economy.

A comparable situation develops when a dairy cooperative which supplies a town with milk has to compete with a businessman who collects only the milk of the farms nearest to the town and seeks to make them leave the cooperative by offering them a higher price while selling more cheaply to the customers of his shop.

DIFFERENTIATION IN TERMS OF CAPACITY FOR PROGRESS

This category includes premiums for quality and for productivity. The so-called quality premium allows a cooperative to pay more for a commodity for which there is a larger or more profitable market while paying less than the market price for products meeting lower standards. It acts as a material stimulus exerting pressure on the farmers to adjust their production to the requirements of the market.

The productivity premium consists in paying more for a given product as soon as the cooperative member achieves a given technical performance or a given output level of animal or vegetable production. It is mainly used to encourage producers to specialize and increase their production volume so as to reduce the cooperative's costs and allow it to use its installations to their full capacity.

In these two cases the differential prices based on capacity for progress are designed to serve the cooperative's need to be competitive as a producer of commodities. They are generally accepted quite readily by the producers, particularly since they are a reward for personal effort. At the same time, however, they widen the gap between the situation of the most advanced and the most backward farmers and may even serve to eliminate those who cannot adjust, gradually but systematically, without offering them either an alternative solution or payment of retraining costs.

DIFFERENTIATION IN TERMS OF QUANTITIES PRODUCED

This is a matter of quantity premiums, or literage premiums in the case of milk, which were introduced by capitalist enterprises and are in some cases applied by cooperatives. They stimulate, for instance, payment of a higher price per liter to the producer whose total output of liters per day is larger. This premium corresponds to the money the enterprise or cooperative can save (mainly on collecting produce) by dealing with large producers.

The literage premium was one of the causes which precipitated the milk war of 1972 in several regions in France, particularly in the west.

CONCLUSIONS

If we ask again how differential prices are accepted by the producers, we see that different forms of discrimination have a different impact on those concerned.

Inequalities linked to technical success are generally accepted quite readily, particularly quality premiums; productivity premiums, however, produce some reservations. It seems that the development of an order of rank based on technical success is not sufficient to break up a community as long as it is still possible to believe in equality of chance.

Discrimination in terms of distance is felt as lack of cooperative solidarity by the unfavorably located producers, who regard it as an injustice, but they reluctantly go along with it when they are not in the majority in the cooperative because they have no alternative solution, and perhaps also because their neighbors are in the same situation.

Quantity premiums, however, often have an explosive effect, because they make it evident to the bulk of the small producers that their cooperative is really at the beck and call of a few privileged members and no longer remains a cooperative project. *

---

*A significant example: once they had made their cooperative stop paying quantity premiums, the producers also rejected the reintroduction of the quality premiums to which they had previously agreed.

This brings us to the more basic question which the practice of differential prices forces us to ask ourselves: is discrimination between producers compatible with the aims of cooperation or not?

An answer to that question is meaningful only with reference to the cooperative village community (in the sense meant by Yair Levi[*]) which the cooperative institution helps to encourage.

In other words differential prices should be used only to the extent that they help build up a cooperative village community in the region. As things are, one cannot help noting that differential prices are more often than not a disruptive factor for the developing cooperative community. They reflect the pressure of the capitalist environment on the rural society; and the ability of the country to resist domination by the town is weakened rather than strengthened as a result. To increase the inequality between the producers rather than to try to reduce it clearly means taking the risk of undermining cooperative solidarity.

It is thus evident that there is indeed such a thing as a struggle between two development projects, and it is an illusion to believe that one can escape the dilemma by such a simple means as honest, competent and so-called efficient management, which more often than not is a carbon copy of that of dynamic capitalistic enterprises.

In reality the problem is not merely of an economic nature, and the cooperatives cannot fight the system's rules of the game on their own. Either they let themselves be forced into practices which conform to the logic of progress by elimination, while justifying such behavior by an appeal to "dynamism" and "efficiency" or collective action by the farmers of the region is necessary, whether they are cooperative members or not, in order to force a change of the rules of the game which capitalistic as well as cooperative enterprises will have to obey.

When economic power reaches its limits the cooperative development project must be defended by trade union power. The cooperatives can play a decisive role in this, if one fully accepts that the cooperative is not just the property of its members but an instrument of collective progress, and that the totality of the workers in the region are its concern.

The solidarity in agitation of the producers in the recent conflicts may have contributed to the growth of this consciousness, but that does not spare us the need for an educational effort to highlight the need for solidary development.

---

[*]See Yair Levi's contribution in this volume: "A Definition of the Rural Cooperative Community in Developing Countries."

NOTE

1. For the role in evolution of struggle and mutual aid, respectively, see Pierre Kropotkin's still topical <u>L'Entraide</u> (Paris: Hachette, 1906).

6

**RURAL REGIONAL
COOPERATION IN ISRAEL**
Yehuda H. Landau

CHANGES AND CHALLENGES
LEADING TO REGIONAL COOPERATION

At the inception of statehood there hardly existed a hierarchical
system of settlements in Israel. Rural settlements attempted to be to
a high degree self-sufficient in regard to local services, and for all
other purposes were mainly linked to two cities, Tel-Aviv and Haifa,
(Jerusalem had no rural hinterland) with hardly any structural linkage
to regional nodes or centers.

From the beginning of independence it has been the long-standing
and undisputed policy of the government to disperse the growing population; this necessitated the development of small new towns throughout the country in order to create balanced regions through an integrated
hierarchical structure of interdependent urban and rural settlements.

Mass settlement of new immigrants from underdeveloped countries
made it imperative that devoted and skilled veterans should also settle
and live in the new regions.

Ways and means had to be found for the integration of the various
ethnic groups and communities.

In the 1950s basic changes in the conditions for agricultural production became apparent. Instead of food shortage and food rationing
there were surpluses. The maxim of increasing production regardless
of cost, in order to feed the population which had trebled in a few years,
had to give way to a drive for efficiency. Diversified farming began to
change into specialized farming, with special emphasis on agricultural
export. The rising standard of living created a demand for better
quality, which required, among other things, adequate sorting and
packing. All this, in conjunction with technological progress, increased

the necessity for economic services and enterprises, which—because
of economies of scale—could not be established in each village. This
was especially the case with the introduction of new crops like cotton,
sugar-beets, peanuts, and vegetables and fruits for processing and
export. All these required new agro-industrial developments. The
problem of surpluses called for new storage and cooling establishments in order to spread the marketing of seasonable-perishable
produce over the whole year, as well as for the development of a
processing industry for such things as juices, canned vegetables and
fruits, frozen and dried products. The expansion and diversification
of agricultural production called for new agro-supporting industries
such as feed mills.

THE DEVELOPMENT OF RURAL REGIONAL
COOPERATION AND ITS OBJECTIVES

Rural settlement in Israel has been based from the start on cooperation, leading to the Kibbutz, the Moshav, and the Moshav Shitufi.
This cooperation at the community level—backed by countrywide apex
organizations—developed not only from the social and ideological aspirations of the settlers, but as a result of the difficulties of adaptation
to a new way of life under very adverse circumstances. Mutual help
was essential to meet these difficulties, as well as for the achievement of economic efficiency and rational organization of the indispensable supporting system.

But this cooperation at the community and national level was not
enough to meet the new challenges and changes. These called for a
further development, termed Rural Regional Cooperation.

Rural Regional Cooperation developed in stages and had its
roots in early beginnings. The first stage started after World War I,
in the field of municipal activities under the British Mandatory Regime.
The then widely dispersed and isolated settlements had to meet common
problems like security and communications, and established for that
purpose committees of groups of settlements in the various regions.
The committees organized these activities and represented the settlements before the mandatory administration and as before the "Jewish
Agency." From these committees developed the system of Rural
Regional Councils, which are today the officially recognized municipal
bodies of the rural regions, each comprising 10-30 settlements.
They are composed of elected representatives, one from each settlement. They are responsible for local government, municipal services,
and the organization and activization of services and institutions for

the development of economic, social, cultural and educational facilities, and they represent their regions in all public affairs.

The second stage started at the beginning of World War II, with the establishment of Regional Purchasing Organizations, which provided the settlements with inputs for production and consumption purposes so that they would not be at the mercy of traders with regard to prices, credit, and quality. These Regional Purchasing Organizations developed into powerful financial instruments in all the rural regions in Israel.

The present stage started in the 1950s with the establishment of regional services and enterprises, to meet two objectives:

First to develop and improve the standard of public services such as education, health, and entertainment—which could not be provided at an adequate level at reasonable cost, in each settlement of 80-100 families. By combining these services for a number of settlements in a rural service center the creation of a social and cultural gap between town and country could be avoided. In these centers suitable conditions could also be maintained for the residence and employment of trained personnel, who were able to serve as the activating and guiding elements so badly needed in modern rural development.

Second, to assist in the absorbtion of new immigrants from less developed countries in the modern social organization of rural Israel. The Planners of rural settlement in Israel arrived originally at this system of rural service centers, in the search for solutions to problems which arose with the settlement of new immigrants from traditional societies. Experience had shown that the separation of the newly arrived family clans and the settlement of families of different origin in one settlement led to ceaseless friction and disputes which endangered the existence of the community. It hindered development of leadership from within, hampered attempts to promote self-management, and wasted energies on local feuds. The most stable settlements were those in which traditional ties had been preserved and in which the settlers had been united from the start by common origin. The feeling of closeness and unity proved to be of great assistance in their adaptation to the new conditions and in the establishment of a community based on mutual aid and responsibility.

But the development of such homogenous communities could retard the process of general integration and hamper the transformation of groups from different countries, with different customs, cultures, outlook and standards of education, into one people.

The establishment of a number of settlements, clustered around a common rural service center, made it possible to settle each ethnic group in a separate settlement, while mutual influences between the settlers of different backgrounds developed in the center, where the merging of the various groups has been accomplished. Regional schools are attended by the children from the various settlements, settlers from all villages meet in the center at various consumer and producer services, common interests are created and the different cultures intermingle at social functions and entertainment activities.

Third, to enable groups of settlements to pool their resources in meeting the challenge of technological progress, which requires machinery and installations, the acquisition and maintenance of which are beyond the capacity of a single settlement. This is not only a problem of economies of scale and of investments, but also one of skilled manpower. Modern agricultural enterprises require specially qualified personnel and high-grade technicians and experts; skill must be acquired from different parts of the world and applied properly to local conditions. Only by the joint efforts of a group of settlements can these challenges be met.

Fourth, to establish agro-supporting and processing industries in the rural areas, in cooperative ownership of the local population, in order to increase the income of the farmers through the added value created by such enterprises.

Fifth, to promote the creation of non-farming employment opportunities in the rural areas (occupational mobility, without geographical mobility). Agricultural progress necessitates structural changes; it means specialization, increase of the means of production at the disposal of the individual production unit, together with a decrease in the labor input in direct agricultural production. But this agricultural exodus does not necessarily mean a rural exodus, a decrease in the percentage of the total population of the country living and working in the rural areas. Through integration of agriculture, industry, and services in rural centers, non-farming employment opportunities can be provided in the rural areas to absorb at least part of the surplus labor force locally and prevent its drift from the country to the cities and causing extreme over-urbanization, with all its inherent dangers. Thus social stability of the rural community can be preserved, in spite of necessary structural changes.

Sixth, to prevent conflicts of interests between countrywide organizations which were in danger of becoming bureaucratized and losing contact with local producers. At the regional level a direct link is maintained between producers and enterprises, since representatives of producers in the various branches decide about the development of the enterprises in accordance with their production plans and forecasts.

Seventh, to promote political articulation of the rural society and of the generation of rural power against urban domination.

TYPES OF RURAL CENTERS

Although the rural centers differ in scope and organizational structure, they are all based on two principles. First, they are erected on nationally owned land, leased for that purpose to the Rural Regional Councils. They are under the jurisdiction of these Councils, which means that the farmers decide about their development and management. Second, services and enterprises established in the centers are, for the most part, in cooperative ownership of the settlements and are managed and operated by their members. There are three kinds of centers.

Subregional Village-Group Centers

These centers are relatively small, linking together four to eight settlements. They comprise public services (such as education, health, entertainment) and farm services (such as packing and sorting of agricultural produce and tractor stations). The people working in these centers—teachers, physicians, nurses, technicians, administrators, and the like—generally live in the residential part of the center. The center and the settlements linked to it form a composite rural community.

Regional Centers

These are mainly within the framework of Rural Regional Councils, comprising 10-30 settlements. The following services and enterprises are usually established in these centers:

1. Maintenance and operation of trucks and of heavy agricultural machinery—for example, tractors for earth-moving operations, cotton pickers, machinery for lifting of sugar-beets, and potato pickers. These operations are executed, with the cooperative machinery from the center.

2. Installations for sorting, packing and cold storage of agricultural produce as well as various agricultural enterprises, for example, cotton gins, alfalfa drying plants, poultry slaughterhouses.

3. Various processing plants.

4. Regional schools—primary, secondary, vocational, and adult education.

5. Extension activities.
6. Regional bakeries, laundries, and so on.
7. Sports and entertainment facilities.
8. Municipal services and administration.

These centers are usually non-residential; the people employed in them commute daily from the villages to the center and back or come from nearby towns.

Inter-Regional Centers

These were formed by several Regional Councils for the purpose of establishing enterprises which require a bigger agricultural hinterland because of scale economies, such as slaughterhouses for cattle, feedmills, and various processing industries. These centers comprise only agro-supporting or processing industries and are also non-residential. They are usually located near small towns.

ORGANIZATION OF REGIONAL COOPERATION

Regional enterprises were generally initiated by the Regional Purchasing Organizations and by Regional Councils, which founded development societies for that purpose. Usually the various settlements are partners only in those enterprises which concern their production. Their participation is according to their share in the regional production volume. In some regions all settlements participate in all enterprises with an equal share. There is generally a centralized regional management board for all enterprises, but for each enterprise there is a separate balance sheet, and its daily operations are directed by a separate management. Each enterprise is also guided by a board of farmers engaged in the particular branch, which decides on its operations and development.

Enterprises are run on a non-profit basis. Member settlements are charged for services or paid for agricultural raw material on a cost-basis. But there is, nevertheless, competition and motivation for efficiency, as member-settlements compare the achievement of their enterprises with those of other regions.

All overhead is centralized for all enterprises of the region—for example, bookkeeping, auxiliary services, infrastructure, financial operations, labor policy, advertising, and marketing—thus achieving advantages of agglomeration and economies of scale.

FIGURE 1

Spatial Distribution of Rural Regional Centers

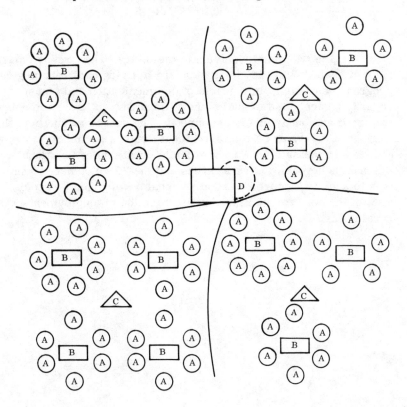

Legend:

(A)   Settlement with local center

[B]   Village group center

△C   Regional center

⌐D⌐   Interregional center

☐E☐   Small town

────   Boundary of rural regional council

Source: Compiled by the author.

Regional Cooperation also forms a link between the farmers and the national apex organizations for marketing and supply.

THE FUTURE

We see two main problems in the future. The first is enlargement of scale. With the rising standard of living and technological progress—especially in the field of communication and transport and regarding economies of scale—the Village Group Centers may become too small and outlive their usefulness. The second is that both the Regional Centers and the Interregional Centers should be more integrated with the small towns in order to create more functional relationships between the rural areas and the "development towns" and thus to achieve a more balanced regional development, especially in view of the need for increased diversification of employment in the rural areas.

**MICRO-REGIONAL
DEVELOPMENT PROJECTS
IN THE FRENCH
RURAL ENVIRONMENT**
Paul Houée

"The pot always starts boiling from the bottom, never from the
top," says an old peasant proverb. The dominant model of a technocratic conception which sees development exclusively as starting from
planning centers and industrial and urban poles is contested by a
multitude of burgeoning local and regional experiments tending to
show that development from below, with its endogenous character,
strong roots and active participation, also has its place and its chance
of succeeding. Groping and ambiguous as these attempts to revitalize
the countryside are, they are a possible breeding ground of new forms
of democratic life, and of collective creativity.

We seek to present here a summary balance sheet of empirical
analyses of eleven such experiments in different parts of France[1] in
order to pave the way for more systematic multi-disciplinary research.
These development projects vary widely in scope (from 2,000 to
450,000 inhabitants), in geographical and economic location (from
deep in the country to the immediate surroundings of the city), and
in origin and type (such as agricultural projects, management studies,
municipal or state initiative). What they have in common is that they
concern small (with one exception) regions in a critical situation, that
their perspective is one of comprehensive development and participation while assigning a place of importance to agriculture, and that they
take place at the meeting point of several local and outside forces.
They may, in the first place, be divided into two main categories.
First there are sectoral projects, mostly initiated by professional
agricultural groups, with a tendency towards the comprehensive development of the region, and with a more or less recognized aim.
Second, there are initiative studies which have a comprehensive
regional development perspective as their point of departure.

Both of these amount to an operations procedure in which one
can generally discern four stages, which are at the same time permanent elements of any development project: gestation of forces and
projects; awakening and crystallization of collective expectations;
organization of action; and management and pursuit of the project.

GESTATION OF FORCES AND PROJECTS

If it is to get off the ground, a locally originated development
project requires three elements. First, it requires a group that
questions its future. Development initiative takes shape in a group
that is coherent and vital enough to take up the challenge of an evolution which disrupts its pattern of organization and existence but feels
disturbed enough to be aware of the need to change. When the group
feels too secure, it is not aware of the need for collective action. If
it is too weak or too severely damaged, it resigns itself to its fate
or expects everything to come from outside.

Second, it requires the emergence of stimulating groupings.
Groups of innovators become the spokesmen of the restlessness of
these threatened groups; they assimilate the new currents of the
large society and the inchoate aspirations and dormant discontent of
the local society.

These groups of innovators often emerge from similar "cultural
seedbeds." It is the Catholic Agricultural Youth (JAC) or similar
groups which provide the initiating teams and the teaching methods of
"seeing-judging-acting," but sometimes it is teachers switching from
vocational education of the young to permanent education of adults, to
leader training or the initial impulse is provided by a charismatic
leader, a cultural or political catalyst. If these groups of innovators
or leaders are to win the support of their environment, they require
the authority due to solid professional success. The groups of members
of the JAC or the Fover Rural (rural home) set up technical groups,
Center d'études techniques agricoles (CETA), or economic organizations (cooperatives, Société d'intérêt collectif agricole or SICA),
before organizing the whole population in a sub-regional committee.
The "equipes de militants et de copains" transform themselves into
teaching networks once their humanistic aims and strategies are
worked out, and a new generation shows by its professional success
that it can give the region elements of a solution which the traditional
powers cannot provide. The group action spreads gradually from
technical problems to comprehensive issues, from farm economy to
the management and development of the entire region, moving from

agricultural to rural and regional matters, such as the creating of jobs, the redistribution of equipment, space management, and the tourist industry. It then becomes necessary to cooperate with other occupations, with local organizations and public authorities, in order to present a joint front to threats from outside and to work out a project for the future of the region. What begins as agricultural action becomes a chapter of micro-regional politics.

Third, it requires the explanation of the possible. Action alone is not enough. If the innovating forces and their aspirations are to join in a collective project, there is need for a study to explore what is possible, to objectify the situation, and to lay the foundations for a reliable future.

The study will obviously take place at the beginning; but it can also take place at other points of the action, in a process of action-research-training-action. Usually the launching of the study is due to the converging of a number of demands from trade union organizations, public authorities and local elected representatives. It bears the mark of those who conduct it, among others "Parisian" national research institutes, which are attractive because of their prestige, references, and relations, but which tend to frighten by their prices, their lack of involvement, and their sometimes technocratic methods. There are also the regional agricultural or university institutes: they are less competent, but closer to the local reality and to those who will be in charge of its evolution.

The study may be called a participation poll, comprehensive diagnosis, or a fact-finding study. Usually it has the same aims: it is intended to be comprehensive by bearing on the entire complex of activities, prospective by formulating future possibilities, and participative by involving elements from the local population.

Generally, one can discern the same stages: contact with all elements involved in order to establish an overall outlook and a coherent view followed by preparation, execution, and evaluation of the study with the assistance of local elected cadres, socio-professional groups, and volunteers. [2]

The study provides a first assessment of forces and potentials, a first forecast of chief assets, possibilities, constraints, and restrictions affecting the viability of the region, and a blueprint for action showing points of support and resistance, growth and stimulation requirements, and the delineation and structure of the field of action.

A population which asks questions about its future, groups of innovators who prove their ability at reconciling specific local conditions and contemporary needs, and studies which define the situation in objective terms and discover a possible horizon are the

factors by which a region begins to recover its identity and put itself
on the road to a possible future.

AWAKENING AND CRYSTALLIZATION
OF COLLECTIVE EXPECTATIONS

There are many rural zones where professional activities and
searching studies have been conducted without any practical effect.
Launching a comprehensive development requires the crossing of a
threshhold in the development of collective consciousness. A new outlook on life, a collective spurt that sets energies free and transforms
latent restlessness into active hope, passivity into a will to live, and
dependence into the emergence of a soundly rooted project is possible
only beyond this threshold.

PATTERNS OF CONSCIENTIZATION

In the 11 projects that have been studied one can discern three
types of conscientization: First, by a continuous development of consciousness without a decisive moment. Most often, the transformation
of a region takes place without sudden spurts or breaks, by a meshing,
a multiplication of small local actions of innovation, which search
each other out, expand their influence, and arouse new aspirations in
a cumulative process of innovations that put the whole countryside
into a state of permanent creativity. The energizing event must in
this case be sought in a deep-lying continuous movement which changes
the look of the countryside peacefully, but from the bottom up, without a specific crisis, but with an accumulation of changes which have
transformed the regional consciousness in depth.
Second, by threatening events. These may be natural events,
such as a flood that destroys a village or the failure of an essential
crop, or socio-economic threats, such as collapse of a local product's
market, the building of a speedway, the construction of a ski resort,
the expansion of an urban zone or military installation. The people
of the countryside react; they feel the threat as an injustice which
they denounce and as an obstacle which can be overcome by their
use of every available energy.
Third, by an initiating study. A study may provide the event
which provokes the reaction of the population. Methods may vary in
different experiments, but the point of departure is always the same;

an overall coherent picture of the situation in the region, and within the region of each place and sector of activity, leading to questions about the future or to meetings of communes with aims which may differ: to elicit a creative reaction of the population without any specific project, to make the population cooperate in a development project sketched in general lines, or to make it join in changes defined by an already finalized project. The operation usually involves a first stage of community meetings open to as wide a public as possible, followed by a few weeks or months in which ideas are allowed to settle down and take shape, often helped along by articles in the press, and finally a stage of resuming action at inter-communal level at which different orientations and working groups emerge.

OUTGROWING THE SITUATION

Thus stimulated, the collective consciousness enters a stage of strong, creative ferment: a breakthrough of imagination and vitality suddenly replaces a determinism that had been taken for granted, raises the level of aspirations, and forces the entire community to depart from the too well-defined pathways of programmed evolution. [3]

The community which had been prevented from knowing and projecting itself, by partial representations and dominant conceptions, is suddenly enabled by a comprehensive, accessible picture of its condition to identify itself, to find itself again in the depths of its threatened being. The study becomes the mirror which shows the population its true image and invites it to take a look at itself. A new, critical view suddenly casts a new light on reality. What was accepted or submitted to as natural becomes less evident, more problematical; the everyday world is illuminated by a new light and an attempt is made to decipher its secrets. One wants to understand one's course of life, to identify the economic, social, cultural, and political processes which explain the present situation.

Space and time supply the essential framework for explanatory comparison in this liberating revelation. Because the local situation is put in relation to other similar situations in which action has been taken, a different future appears possible. Historical analysis puts the actual situation into the context of the people's development through the centuries and restores their awareness of its identity and the will to discover new patterns of expressing it. Only a group which has discovered the meaning of its present through its understanding of its past is capable of inventing its future. [4] Once the habit is broken people find that they have crossed the borderlines of their daily lives.

Everything seems unedited, unforeseeable. "There is nothing to be done" is replaced by "things must change," an entire people starts hoping again, even dreaming. But can there be development without utopia?

Thus revealed, the situation appears to be a challenge for the entire community to take up. This means transforming concern into hope, which is never easy. Insisting too much on local restrictions or on the omnipotence of inaccessible powers may arouse militants but makes the masses despair; overstating possible hopes produces a passing euphoria followed by general disappointment. Confronted with a situation they have not yet read, the active forces of development look to their history for the distinguishing criteria and the aims which justify overcoming it: to develop a region means to give a people back to themselves so that they may achieve their own limits.

The link between past and future is sometimes provided by a charismatic leader who symbolizes recovered identity and proclaimed hope; the rules of the social game demand that he shall have his roots in the countryside but occupy a position in the general society. But there is a difference between the stage of propulsion, when prophetic inspiration is sometimes needed to pull the region out of its inertia, and the stage of gravitation and management when the movement has been put into orbit and is carried along by the entire social system.

Into the breech that has just opened rush the most widely different expectations, from wishes for the immediate future to long-term visions; there often is an expectation of a veritable rain of miraculous subsidies. Initiators must channel and focus aims, targets, means, and action on a comprehensive project. Such a popular movement, arising from and appealing to the emotions, may make skeptics and technocrats smile, but if it is to break its chains and confining walls, if it is to create itself anew, a people needs its Fourth of August.

This catalysis sets unforeseen energies into motion. Gradually, these energies lose their turbulence, and become fixed on a few points of support, active personalities and main directions. The forces which have remained unutilized then rally around a symbol, a slogan, a leader, a still fragile structure. The project is still general and not defined in detail; it is often an accumulation of aims, means and initiatives, arranged in terms of dominant problems or major sectors of activity.

ORGANIZATION OF ACTION

The appearance of new needs and new active personalities, the crystallization of their energies and their projects, calls for sound organization in order to assure the efficacy and continuity of the movement while maintaining a permanent tension between creative ferment and the rule of reason, the comprehensive scope of the basic aspirations and the specificity of the solutions provided. Action takes place through the organization of forces, aims, and powers.

The development action takes shape while remaining at the mercy of alliances and conflicts which arise among the active personalities in an interplay of internal and external forces which always seek to let their aims, norms, and models prevail.

The participation of the population varies with the stages and patterns of intervention. In the continuous development process it allows itself to be won over gradually by the innovators as soon as their success no longer appears as a threat to the environment; the professional leader becomes a public opinion leader and takes his place in a network of relations and connections.

In the intensive processes collective enthusiasm often collapses soon and is replaced by disappointment, impatience, and aggressiveness.

Development action reinforces local cohesion, the horizontal dimension that bridges socio-professional gaps. It is tempting to disregard traditional representatives and to appeal to people who are not yet burdened with official duties, but in most cases experience shows that an operation fails if it does not have the support of the majority of the elected mayors of the region. The initiative then becomes a matter of continuous information and of patient training of local functionaries until some forms of inter-communal cooperation can emerge. Of great importance are organized groups, particularly professional groups and cultural associations, which are the support as much as the beneficiaries of regional awakening. Working commissions bring together municipal functionaries and professionals, elected representatives and volunteers. They are the crossroads where hope becomes a program of action, goodwill turns into a structure of thought and involvement. Some of these commissions are extra-municipal, others have been set up for study purposes or have become permanent structures of the development agency.

The departmental professional organizations do not always find their place in the process; either they control the action, and then the local elected representatives and other socio-professional categories retreat into silence, or they disregard a movement which

disturbs them and escapes their control. Specialized organizations
find it easier to make their specific contribution to a regional undertaking.

The administration is a partner without which no development
action can succeed. [5] This is particularly true for the Department of
Agriculture, which involves itself unobtrusively in the initiative.
Regional missions and national institutions are often favorably in-
clined towards innovating initiatives.

ORGANIZATION OF AIMS AND MEANS

The aim of development action becomes defined in greater depth
when local aspirations and general data are analysed. This is the entire
role of the working commissions, in which local representatives and
experts confront the expectations of the environment and the needs of the
general society. By stepwise approaches and analyses they will usually
achieve dynamic understanding of the reality with its entire environment, until they arrive at a certain consensus which helps each par-
ticipant look beyond his particular horizon. These groups play a rationalizing role by activating an inductive method of socialization and information.

Control of information is essential all through the action: it
means being well connected with sources of skill and authority, making
oneself known and gaining recognition, and acquiring an audience. In
order to obtain the necessary reputation, people engaged in the action
must build up records, approach authorities, make their way in the
workings of the administration, and at the same time initiate actions
which produce activity and then follow them up.

The project must aim at a measure of coherence in order to
meet the general nature of the expectations of the population and to
remain credible in the eyes of outside partners. Thus all projects
seek more and more rigorous programming while adjusting to the
rationalizing models of the decision-making centers. Once the program has been worked out in this manner it must be approved by the
decision-making instances: either the official "Amenagement Rural"
Plan Commission or the appropriate local authorities or professional
organs.

The crystallization of the forces at work and the realization of
the hopes which have been raised depends above all on the consistency
of the micro-regional authority, its ability to work out and carry out
its own strategy, the measure in which it is rooted in the local system,
and its ability to obtain a hearing from other authorities. The renewal

of regional dynamism mostly takes shape around two poles of power: professional and inter-communal, and it is rare for one organization to have its authority acknowledged by all active bodies and communities.

Recognition of micro-regional authority depends on its means, including financial means and their sources, and the activists it employs; its relations with the population and with local groups; the information system between the authority and the local population; and on its relations with outside forces and recognition of the regional identity.

A development operation will always be a gamble, a balance between different or even opposing forces which must constantly be re-established. "Knowhow alone is files lying unused in cabinets; power alone is managing current affairs without foresight; will alone is revolt without a tomorrow."

PURSUIT OF ACTION

Experiments of this kind are too recent and too rare to provide a basis of comparison with the prevailing models of centralized development. At most, one can note certain directions to avoid, and means of circumventing them.

Micro-regional development has nothing in common with the systematic execution of a rigid plan; rather, it is a multiplication of initiatives among which one glimpses certain signs of interlinking and sometimes discerns recognizable coordination. The development action takes the form of a multiplication of individual and collective initiatives; the activity often starts from farm enterprises, takes hold of other occupations and collectives, and spreads to the entire range of activities and sectors of local life. The correlation of these initiatives results in cumulative processes, in new productive combinations, in chain reactions; it creates a general climate of innovation, of communication, of solidarity, a desire to put things right, which stimulates permanent creation, spread and socio-cultural integration of new departures. The micro-regional authority makes its mark on small and medium enterprises but cannot control massive intervention by outside capital; hence the limitations of micro-regional development.

Implementation of the program takes the form of intensification and acceleration of individual professional and municipal implementation, of the continuous development of new projects, of better control of communal budgets, and of inter-communal forecasts. Control of the action is effected to a very minor extent by popular vote and by

the participation of the population in the executing bodies, and to a
greater extent by regular administrative procedure and by study contracts.

Initiating development is still prone to failure. No habitual patterns have yet been developed for it, and it may easily disappoint and
break down because of action through agitation, which fails to make
an impact on actual conditions and therefore escapes into ideological
refinements or into propaganda producing momentary intoxication and
then its aftermath of lassitude; action by way of integration, which
masks conflicts and gives the local forces an illusion of autonomy,
but in effect makes them accept decisions made at another level; or
Institutionalization, in which the development organ becomes an aim
in itself.

If the strain of any innovating action and the encroachment of a
system which absorbs anything that deviates are to be resisted constant
renewal is imperative. Some experiments content themselves with replacing their management by means of the usual game of elections at
municipal and professional organization level; others accept the existence of permanent tension between decision-making structures and
parallel groups. The revision of objectives and the evaluation of
actions is often formalized in reports and general meetings. The most
effective renewal results in actions which set forces in movement and
each time involve larger strata of the population in a process of
change; it results to an even greater extent from a permanent formation which, in response to questions arising from the action, adjusts
itself at the appropriate moment in accordance with the rhythm of
the action.

In a summary such as this analysis of a few development actions,
it is sufficient to bring out certain problems of endogenous development. Are these the throes of village societies mobilizing their last
energies and illusions on the borders of a current which will merci-
lessly sweep them away? Or are they the sprouting of new forms of
democratic life and social regulation, the annunciation of something
surpassing our rational civilizations in the direction towards more
liberty, creativity, and solidarity in real life? We cannot yet en-
visage clearly how such collective conscience and will, once it has
gained new strength, will be able to hold its own against the promoters of economic organizations and the managers of space. At any
rate these experiments show that a people armed with a few techniques
and good communications can define the future which is within its
reach and can put energies and means to work which surpass the more
classical actions of professional and civic groups while encompassing
them. One may say that it is utopian to believe a population capable of
conceiving its own future and mastering its own activities and hopes;

but that means forgetting that while the light comes usually from on high, the sap always rises from deep below. The regional societies have no solution other than to make this collective start in order to promote their identity and liberty: this is their tragedy, but also their chance.

NOTES

1. Pic St-Loup (Hérault): 3 cantons, 17 communes, 7,500 inhabitants, 1960; Champsaur (Hautes Alpes): 3 cantons, 29 communes, 9,250 inhabitants, 1958; Haute-Morienne (Savoie): 8 communes, 2,314 inhabitants, 1955; Crolles and Grésivaudan (Isère) 42 communes, 60,000 inhabitants, 1943; St. Lézin and Chemillé (Maine-et-Loire): 1 canton, 18 inhabitants, 1950; Ploudalmézeau (Finistère): 1 canton, 10 communes, 13,000 inhabitants, 1966; St-Florent-le-Viel (Maine-et-Loire): 11 communes, 13,700 inhabitants, 1966; Mené (Côtes du Nord): 16 communes, 20,000 inhabitants, 1966; Pévéle-Mélantois (Nord): 36 communes, 1963; Haut-Nivernais-Clamecy (Nièvre): 1 arrondissement, 73 communes, 33,400 inhabitants, 1970; Semenf (Nord-Finistère): 168 communes, 450,000 inhabitants, 1963. (The date indicates the year in which the experiment started, as far as can be established.)

2. R. Catllot, L'enquête participation, méthodologie de l'aménagement. (Paris: Ed. Ouvrières, 1973).

3. H. Desroche, Sociologie de l'espérance (Paris: Calmann-Lévy, 1973).

4. P. Houee, Les étapes du développement rural, 2 vols. (Paris: Ed. Ouvrières, 1972).

5. J.P. Worms, "Le préfet et ses notables," Sociologie du Travail (March 1966).

AGRICULTURAL COOPERATION, REGIONAL DEVELOPMENT, AND THE PROMOTION OF FARMERS
Médard Lebot

The following are some selected remarks on a multi-purpose agricultural cooperative in western France, "Cooperative Agricole la Noelle, Ancenis" (CANA).

ATTITUDES OF FARMERS TO COOPERATIVES

In western France the types of farmers in cooperatives fall into four categories, sociologically speaking. In the first are the farmers who, jealous of their own freedom, their business as well as their private sector, are resistant to cooperative ideology; in the second are farmers who are cooperators either by conviction or because no alternative to cooperation exists in their region. The CANA cooperators are mainly of this kind. The third category consists of active trade unionists, usually young and struggling farmers who turn to cooperation when it pays them to do so, but who can come into conflict with their cooperative in the course of their fight for survival. And the fourth is a new type of big business entrepreneur who, while having interests which conflict with those of the cooperative, and tending to stand aloof from it, does get out of it what he can.

Faced with this kind of situation, the cooperative movement in the western part of France is hard put to maintain and develop its original objective to play a key role in regional development and to act as a means of participation, information, and formation to the farmers who opt for cooperation.

MULTI-PURPOSE COOPERATIVES
AND REGIONAL AGRICULTURAL DEVELOPMENT

Despite the great difficulties encountered by cooperatives in France, which are aggravated by strong international competition, they continue to play a part in regional agricultural development.

Location of Agricultural Production in Specific Regions

Cooperatives are contained in one agricultural area. In event of their proving unlucrative, they never relocate in another region, preferring to disappear or to be absorbed in some similar enterprise.

An example is to be found in the pea-canning industry in Brittany, which constituted 70-80 percent of the total production for France 15 years ago, as against 20 percent today. This was the result of the relocation of the industry to the Paris region on the part of private firms actuated by purely economic motives. The cooperatives never relocated, having either modernized, merged, or closed down altogether.

A further example is to be found in the construction in 1958 by CANA of a creamery at Ancenis, an agricultural region noted for cattle raising and meat production. There was much criticism against cooperative investment of this kind at the time. Agricultural expertise maintained that what was needed was a meat factory and not a creamery. Thanks to the intelligent direction of those in charge of the cooperative, the plant soon proved too small so that in 1969, another plant had to be constructed, this time equipped with a spray tower which had a 30,000 litre per hour capacity. Milk production in the CANA region increased considerably as a result. The number of cooperative producers grew from 5,360 in 1960 to 7,290 in 1972, with the annual average output per producer soaring from 8,167 litres to 30,272 litres.

Collective investment on a regional scale was thus proved beneficial to milk production in the CANA region. The farmers realized that, assured of a profitable outlet, they could increase production. The collective investment and conversion involved proved a key factor in the development of agricultural production and economy of an entire region.

Thanks to its polyvalence, the Ancenis Cooperative was able to take the risk of engaging in the Enterprise in 1958. It was its older more established sectors, such as cereals and supplies, which made

it possible to take the risk of investing in the creamery, a situation
which is inverted today, with the creamery providing the backing for
ventures in meat production.

It must be pointed out that numerous agricultural regions un-
involved in multi-purpose cooperatives have experienced serious contraction in their agricultural economy. The efficiently managed polyvalent cooperatives have, on the other hand, had a key role in regional
development and in the location of production.

Development of Processing and Farmers' Incomes

For private firms with country-wide connections a loss in any
particular region stands to be recovered elsewhere. Many farmers
under contract to such firms have discovered to their dismay that
while the risks are all theirs, the profits are not, and often have had
recourse to trade union action as their only defence in case of need.
Only recently the Trade Union movement in Loire-Atlantique has come
out in defense of one such young farmer, in debt by about 150,000
francs (about $30,000 in 1974).

A multi-purpose and highly industrialized cooperative must base
its development on equally industrialized units of production. It cannot
afford to employ modern industrial means of production in its larger
undertakings while restricting its farmers to an artisan level of production. The cooperative is obliged to do all in its power to help its
members benefit from the processes of industrialization.

Assertions of this kind are strengthened by the fact that in the
Ancenis area where the CANA multi-purpose cooperative is strongly
entrenched there are more bids for enterprises offered on the market
than there are in the Redon area where the cooperative movement has
just started to penetrate. In addition, land prices are higher in cooperative areas, since the farmers there are more advanced and
successful.

The more any particular form of production develops in any one
region, the more it tends to endure, and to expand. An atmosphere
favorable to the idea of organization is thus created, a fact illustrated
by the case of the creamery cooperatives of the western region and
the pork producer groups of Brittany, both of which made a considerable contribution in their respective fields of production, while at the
same time giving the farmers confidence to withstand those who opposed them in fear of overproduction.

Moral Support through Solidarity for Farmers

The independent farmer sees his chances for survival increase
with his belonging to a group. Cooperation offers him a means of
coming to terms with the forces of progress which might otherwise
submerge him.

In the cooperative at Ancenis, the specialized producers group
together to decide on the directions suitable to their respective pro-
ductions. While it is the Administrative Council which fixes objectives
and suggests ways and means, it is up to the producers themselves,
operating within their specialized groups, to decide on the implementation of the policy mapped out for them.

The action of the last annual general meeting of the calf breeders
is one case in point. In order not to discourage breeders it was decided not to make membership conditional on the acceptance of any
basic minimum unit of production. Rather than impose the rigid scale
operating in the large plants, the cooperative producers chose to proceed on the basis of financial results, in directing their breeders
towards a remunerative industrialized veal-producing plant. A maximum, difficult to achieve, was fixed for the region by the Administrative Council of the CANA regarding criteria of full employment,
profits, and economic and technical factors. In this case it was the
producers themselves who decided on the type of enterprise to promote, thereby creating for themselves a sense of solidarity and a
belief in the future.

FARMERS' PARTICIPATION
IN AGRICULTURAL COOPERATIVES

Faced with present-day industrial expansion in the food and
agricultural industries of France and of Europe, the cooperative movement has no hope of getting anywhere unless it improves the quality
of its managerial personnel, supports development among its farmers,
and persuades the authorities to give concrete expression to their policy
of backing the cooperative movement in agriculture.

Even if these conditions are satisfied the struggle of cooperatives will persist, confronted as it is with the formidable national and
international competition of food and agricultural industries.

As to the improvement of the human potential, this can be
achieved by closer attention to recruitment and to scientific approaches,
and to better pay. Results will not be slow to follow.

The support of the authorities for the cooperative movement can only be obtained by political means and through the efforts of the farmers themselves. At this level the trade unions and the cooperatives have to form a common front, not just to preserve intact existing gains, but to clarify the objectives in order that cooperation may play a key role in agricultural development.

A certain amount of imagination is called for on the part of those in charge of the cooperatives so that the farmers in discharging organizational and promotional functions do so in such a way as to command confidence. It is the latter point which will be dwelt upon in what follows.

Structures of Participation in Cooperatives

In an expanding cooperative the center of decision-making tends to move away from the farmer, president and director alike becoming less accessible. This creates a gulf between the management and the cooperators, so that members can find themselves reduced to the level of clients.

This situation can be remedied only by the farmers being encouraged to confront the problems facing their cooperative, a possibility conditional on the goodwill of the administrative council and the management.

The CANA's scale of operations, which covers an area of 100 kilometers, showed an increase of 23 percent in 1972 over that of 1971. This increase has continued to the present, with a turnover of about 600 million new francs (about $120 million) and 30,000 cooperators.

Every effort is made to render the structures of participation as dynamic as possible, and to facilitate their renovation when necessary.

The CANA is managed by an administrative council of 26 members, elected annually, all of whom are farmers, who meet once a month at least. After the Annual General Meeting this council elects a bureau of eight. Certain administrators are delegated to preside over "particular commissions" created by the Council relating to social operations, distribution marketing, cooperative promotion, livestock production, and finance.

The CANA is recognized as a Producers' Group with regard to certain of its activities. The farmers concerned meet several times during the year and delegate representatives to the commissions of the specialized groups, whose function is to refer proposals to the Administrative Council.

In consideration of the large number of members and their wide-spread dispersal, large numbers of representatives maintain contact between the cooperators and the Administrative Council. They meet at least once per trimester. Their opinions and suggestions are seriously evaluated.

In 1972, the Council divided the CANA zone into ten promotional sectors, with a delegated administrator responsible for cooperative activity at the head of each. There is at present an attempt to establish "zone committees" made up of representatives of zones and specialized groups. The emergent organization is vertical as to production and horizontal as to sector or zone.

The number of cooperators delegated to undertake responsibilities in the cooperative is estimated at about 1,000.

Information and Formation of Cooperators

The Annual General Meetings and other meetings of regional polyvalent cooperatives do not constitute an adequate source of information for members. Not more than 3,000 approximately, out of a total of 30,000 cooperators, take part in the sectional annual meetings of the CANA. It is true that there is a paper and a monthly information sheet circulated among members supplying detailed information about particular problems. But written information has a limited impact in a peasant area, for farmers are not readers. Oral information, therefore, would be preferable, if it were not for three difficulties: First, farmers cannot be relied upon for attendance at meetings—a maximum of 20-30 percent of those invited usually come. Second, the background level of farmers varies widely so that there is a language problem which accounts for the absence of certain of the more important farmers at meetings. Third, individual oral information involves the employment of means not readily available on all occasions.

There are, however, two techniques which could be conveniently employed in a peasant environment. The first is audio-visual communication. Information presented through television or slide-projectors is certainly more readily assimilable under such circumstances. The second is study tours, which could be introduced in the slack season for the dispersal of information.

CONCLUSIONS

First, agricultural cooperatives, no matter how important and
efficient, cannot be the sole means of carrying out regional development, which is a global matter and must involve the entire environment. Nevertheless, polyvalent cooperatives on a regional scale can
play a key role in agricultural development as far as the improvement
of farmers' incomes and their general prospects are concerned.

Second, the cooperatives likely to suceed in the face of increasing economic competition are those which have a satisfactory
financial basis and have the ability of making the maximum use of
innovations.

Third, cooperatives are by their nature a favored means of
promotion for an agricultural environment. They have an advantage
over private firms in that they can place full confidence in the farmers.
This being so, the circulation of information and the decentralization
of responsibility are priorities to which the group intelligence and
imagination must be directed.

Fourth, in the words of J. Le Bihan, "In this struggling world,
power and initiative belong to those who possess the best information
and use it in decision-making." But can information and formation be
separated in the case of the character creation of cooperative farmers?
If the one must be concrete and comprehensive, the other can only be
possible in investing men with responsibility and shared power, in
equipping them with a new language which will transform them from
submissive into understanding humans.

PART

III

INDUSTRIALIZATION
OF RURAL AREAS

9

ECONOMIC DIVERSIFICATION IN ISRAELI VILLAGES
Samuel Pohoryles

THE RELATIONSHIP BETWEEN FARMING AND NON-FARMING IN THE RURAL ECONOMY

A study of population censuses and annual manpower surveys carried out by the Central Bureau of Statistics indicates the structural changes which have taken place in the Israeli village in the course of the last 25 years:

TABLE 9.1

Changes in the Economic Structure of the Israeli Village
(number of workers employed, in percent)

	1948	1970	1973
Agriculture, afforestation, and fishing	56.9	43.3	36.8
Industry	11.8	14.3	14.6
Electricity and water	—	0.4	0.1
Building and public works	3.0	2.2	11.8
Transport, storage, and communications	3.2	4.0	4.2
Commerce, banking, and insurance	2.2	3.0	9.4
Public and business services	8.2	22.3	14.5
Personal services and recreation	14.7	10.5	8.6
Total	100.0	100.0	100.0

Source: Israel Statistical Yearbooks, 1971 and 1974;
Population Registration 1949, Central Bureau of Statistics, Jerusalem.

There has been a decline in the place of agriculture in the economy of the village during the last 25 years—from 57 percent to 37 percent of the total number of workers in the village. Agriculture is still the most important and decisive branch in the Israeli rural economy. In fact, quite a number of workers employed in other branches of the economy are actually servicing agriculture: for example, the transport branch includes the haulage of agricultural produce and the building branch covers the construction of agricultural buildings and the execution of repairs and improvements.

The data given in the table indicate a large increase in public services. The reason for this lies in the considerable expansion of education, health services, and the various municipal services in the village. There has also been a certain increase in the percentage of workers employed in industry and trades. The larger proportion of public services and industry testify to the process of modernization which is taking place in the village and to its adaptation to the economic patterns of today. There is no doubt that these processes have been a factor in fortifying the village and increasing its ability to face up to the pressures of urbanization, while simultaneously laying the foundations for the integration of agriculture and industry.[1]

Non-agricultural employment in the village enables the farmer to supplement his income from agriculture. The Israeli village is capable of creating additional sources of employment and income. A number of problems connected with "economies of scale" arise since the development of industry and services requires a certain minimal dimension in production units. The Kibbutz solves this problem within its own organizational unit; the Moshav can find a solution only through intra-regional rural cooperation, and in order to achieve this end, it has to overcome a large number of organizational and social obstacles.[2]

It should be mentioned that diversification of employment in the village also creates other important economic and social changes quite apart from sources of income. A relatively large concentration of services in the village enables the inhabitants to enjoy the conveniences of urban life. A survey of living conditions made in 1969 (Central Bureau of Statistics, Publications Series No. 323, Jerusalem) showed that 99.6 percent of rural Jewish families use electricity. The parallel percentage in town was 99.8 percent. One hundred percent of both urban and rural families enjoy running water. The housing density coefficient was 1.7 persons per room in the village as against 1.4 in town. It is also of interest to note the data on domestic equipment in rural homes of Jewish families: in 1969, 96 percent of rural Jewish families used gas for cooking and baking, as against 90.3 percent in town; 59.1 percent of rural families had washing machines as compared with 40.4 percent in town; 91.1 percent village families had

radios, as against 90.6 percent in town; 15.9 percent had private cars
as against 14.9 percent of urban families; 33.5 percent had television
sets in the village and 31.8 percent in town; 93.9 percent had electric
refrigerators in the village as against 94.9 percent in town. The rural
population also enjoys extensive facilities in the field of culture and
entertainment, such as lectures, libraries, exhibitions, theatre, and
a high standard of educational services. It should also be noted that
urban ways of life exert a considerable influence on the patterns of
village life, and this is a factor which encourages the introduction and
development of industry within the village. Industrialization in single
settlements, and even more within the broader framework of regional
cooperation, enables the village to keep up to a large extent with the
pace of urban development insofar as the standard of living is concerned.

The development foreseen for the coming 10-15 years will bring
about a further decline in the importance of agriculture—and to some
extent also of services—in the village, while there will be a substantial
rise in the part played by industry. It may be assumed that around the
year 1980 there will be the following proportions in the distribution of
workers employed in the Israeli village: agriculture—40 percent; industry, including electricity, water and building—30 percent; services,
including commerce and transport—30 percent.

INDUSTRIALIZATION IN THE KIBBUTZ

In the Kibbutz economy, industry already accounts for close to
30 percent of the total net product. There are now Kibbutzim in which
the contribution of industry to the net product is identical with that of
agriculture. The data in the following table show the changes that have
taken place in the Kibbutz in its progress towards integration of agriculture and industry since the establishment of the state.

The dynamic pace of development in the Kibbutzim points to a
number of important issues. The percentage of agriculture dropped
from 55.4 percent in the year 1948 to 30.7 percent in 1973. Industry
(including electricity and water) rose from 9.7 percent to 20.5 percent in 1973. Services, including commerce, transport, and hauling,
rose from 33 percent in 1948 to 47.0 percent in 1973. An interesting
fact should be emphasized: the rate of development of Kibbutz industry
was more rapid than that of industry in the state in general. This may
be seen from the data in Table 9.3.

TABLE 9.2

Distribution of Workers in Kibbutzim According
to Economic Branches, 1948-73
(in percent)

	1948	1961	1966	1968	1969	1970	1973
Agriculture, afforestation, and fishing	55.4	44.0	38.0	36.1	36.7	31.6	30.7
Industry	—	17.7	18.5	19.1	18.3	17.4	20.4
Electricity, and water	9.7	0.4	0.1	0.1	0.3	0.2	0.2
Building and public works	1.9	3.5	1.3	1.9	1.5	1.4	1.8
Transport, storage, and communication	2.6	4.7	3.4	3.6	4.7	4.6	2.9
Commerce, banking, and insurance	0.5	0.5	0.4	0.4	0.1	—	11.5
Public services	9.6	12.6	14.8	14.4	11.9	44.8	11.8
Personal services and recreation	20.3	16.6	23.5	24.4	26.5	—	20.8
Total	100.0	100.0	100.0	100.0	100.0	100.0	100.0

Source: Israel Statistical Yearbooks, 1971 and 1974; Population
Registration 1949, Central Bureau of Statistics, Jerusalem.

TABLE 9.3

Development of Kibbutz Industry
as Compared to Overall Industrialization

	1960	1965	1967	1970	1974
Number employed in Kibbutz industry	6,450	10,368	12,898	14,408	18,298
Number employed in Israeli industry	162,200	222,792	203,800	234,000	252,900
Kibbutz industrial workers as percentage of all workers in Israeli industry	4.0	4.7	6.3	6.2	7.2

Sources: 1960—estimate based on Histadrut Industry censuses; 1965—Trades
and Industry Census 1965; 1967—S. Reich, Development of Kibbutz Industry, Economic
Quarterly, (December 1968): 59-60; 1970—Data of the Union of Kibbutz Industry; and
1974—Data of the Union of Kibbutz Industry.

86

While the number of workers employed in Kibbutz industry rose by 184 percent in the years 1960-74, the increase in the whole of Israeli industry rose by about 56 percent. Consequently, the percentage of workers in Kibbutz industry, as against the overall number working in industry rose from four percent to 7.2 percent.

The dynamic pace of development of industry in the Kibbutzim will be made even clearer in a longterm breakdown:

TABLE 9.4

Number of Workers in Kibbutz Industrial Enterprises
and in Other Settlement Forms in Israel, 1952-74

Form of Settlement	1952	1965	1974
Kibbutzim	3,654	10,368	18,298
Other forms of rural settlement	3,653	8,060	11,000*
Urban settlements	88,906	195,619	223,602

*estimate.

Sources: Enterprises engaged in industry according to "HaYishuv," May 1965; Publications of Industry and Trades No. 4 (Jerusalem: Central Bureau of Statistics, 1967): 38; Census of Industry (Jerusalem: Bureau of Statistics, 1954, 1967, and 1974).

These figures show that from 1952-74 the number of people employed in industry in the Kibbutz increased nearly five-fold. It also emerges that, among the various settlement forms in Israel, the most rapid rate of industrial growth took place in the kibbutz.

The net product of the Kibbutzim in the year 1969 fell into three main categories: agriculture, 42 percent; industry, including trades and building, 34 percent; and services, including commerce, banking, transport, and others, 24 percent.

According to a forecast carried out by the statistical departments of the various Kibbutz movements, in the year 1975 there will be an increase in the available manpower in Kibbutzim of some 12,400 people. Of this number, only 2,250 will be employed in agriculture; somewhat more than 82 percent of the additional workers will have to be absorbed in non-agricultural branches. This development will broaden the diversity of the Kibbutz economy and the internal streamlining among the various branches. It will also increase the need for an expansion of the economic system of the Kibbutz into a regional framework.

The requirement of larger production units adjusted to meet the challenges of modern technology and of competition on world markets makes it necessary to extend this process, which will also lead to a more rational utilization of the existing potential.

THE MAIN COMPONENTS OF THE MOSHAV ECONOMY

The main components which make up the Moshav economy and the changes in internal relations within the Moshav may be seen in the following table, which outlines the economic structure of the Moshav during the period of the last 25 years:

TABLE 9.5

Distribution of Workers in Moshavim
According to Economic Branches 1948-73
(in percent)

	1948	1961	1966	1968	1969	1970	1971
Agriculture, afforestation, and fishing	65.7	72.6	71.4	69.3	66.6	66.2	58.4
Industry	10.7	3.9	6.0	7.9	8.0	7.8	9.9
Water and electricity	—	0.3	0.3	1.0	0.5	0.5	0.2
Building and public works	3.1	3.2	2.2	1.5	0.9	2.3	4.0
Transport, haulage, storage, and communications	2.4	1.4	2 5	2.3	2.7	2.7	4.1
Commerce, banking, and insurance	3.6	3.5	3.4	3.0	4.1	—	4.4
Public and business services	14.5	13.0	12.5	12.3	14.3	20.5	15.7
Personal services and recreation	—	2.1	1.7	2.7	2.9	—	3.3
Total	100.0	100.0	100.0	100.0	100.0	100.0	100.0

Source: Israel Statistical Yearbooks, Central Bureau of Statistics, Jerusalem, for each year listed above.

These figures indicate that even today agriculture still employs 58.4 percent of all Moshav workers, which is the highest percentage in all forms of agricultural settlement. This proportion has only slightly decreased from 1948. The process of structural changes is slow in the Moshav since it encounters greater difficulties than does the Kibbutz.

In order to evaluate the reasons for these difficulties the fact
should be taken into account that, from the point of view of industrial
development, (or of haulage, building, and other enterprises), the
situation of the Moshavim is inferior to that of the Kibbutzim. In the
Kibbutz the collective is in a position to set up industrial or other
undertakings, while the Moshavim have not yet set up any framework
which is able to take over any widespread industrialization activity.
Recently certain changes may be noticed in this field. Thus, for example, the regional councils have also become a factor which can
accelerate industrial development in the Moshav.

Moshav agriculture itself will give a certain impetus in the
direction of diversifying Moshav employment. The agricultural family
unit in its classic form suffers from structural weakness today.
Solutions in the direction of creating optimal production standards and
the creating of conditions for the absorption of manpower freed from
agricultural work occur on two levels: First, within the Moshav itself
by a new form of internal allocation of production factors and by changes
in capital-labor relationships and in the structure of cooperation; and
second, on the regional level—in the framework of cooperative regional undertakings—integrating the Moshavim in inter-Moshav or
joint Moshav-Kibbutz economic systems dealing with overall economic
development.

It cannot be said that the requirements of modernization contra-
dict the principles of the Moshav—the opposite is true. The orientation of the modern farm economy reinforces the central principle of
cooperation and of strengthening ties with the cooperative in all matters
connected with development, in order to lead up to the effective economic integration of the agricultural family unit and the economic
contribution of non-agricultural branches in the village and on the
regional plane. This will produce a model of a family farm as part of
the regional cooperative organization in which agriculture holds a
more important place than in other types of settlement but will, nevertheless, not constitute the only branch within it. This development
will also enable the Moshav to solve the social problems of the second
and third generations, some of whom are liable to leave the village
for town life if no diversified professional employment pattern is
evolved.

TRENDS IN RURAL PLANNING—
PREVENTION OF RURAL POPULATION DECLINE BY
DIVERSIFICATION OF EMPLOYMENT

The following table shows that parallel with the decline of agriculture in the Israeli economy in the last six years there has also been
a decline in the proportion of the rural population to total population.

TABLE 9.6

Changes in the Percentage of Agricultural Workers
and of Rural Population in Israel, 1957-69

Year	Agricultural Workers Percentage of Total Israeli Workers (1)	Rural Population as Percentage of Total Israeli Population (2)	Coefficient of Villag Agriculture Proport (2) (3) = (1)
1957	17.2	24.2	1.4
1959	16.4	23.6	1.4
1961	17.1	22.1	1.3
1963	14.3	20.2	1.4
1965	13.0	18.1	1.4
1966	12.4	18.3	1.5
1968	10.4	17.8	1.7
1969	9.7	17.5	1.8
1970	8.8	17.4	2.0
1973	7.5	16.6	2.2

Source: Israel Statistical Yearbooks, Central Bureau of Statistics,
Jerusalem, for the years 1957-74.

We see, therefore, that with the lower percentage of workers
employed in agriculture in Israel (from 17.2 percent in 1957 to 7.5
percent in 1973) there was a parallel drop in the proportion of the
rural population to the total population (from 24.2 percent to 16.6
percent).

From this we may deduce an important fact: if the decline of the
place of the rural areas in the overall population of the country is to
be prevented or at least slowed down, there is no way other than to
strengthen the village economy. Strengthening the village economy
today is possible only by diversifying the economic branches and
sources of employment within it. This holds good both for agriculture
and for industry and the various service branches. First and foremost, therefore, there must be an allocation of means for the promotion of industrialization in the Moshav, since this type of settlement is seriously backward in its industrial development. The village
economy should also be directed to such ends as setting up tourist
services and transport and haulage projects.

IMPORTANCE OF ECONOMIC-TECHNICAL INFRASTRUCTURE

The infrastructure in general and the economic-technical infrastructure in particular are of great importance in diversifying the village economy. The principal components of the latter infrastructure are water, electricity, road network, means of transport, and buildings required. There are a number of natural factors, such as the uneven geographical distribution of water resources and of arable land and topographical conditions, which have determined the need for the development of an extensive, state-financed water infrastructure. This infrastructure is countrywide and constitutes a ramified inter-regional system serving both town and village. It was this infrastructure which, in the past, determined to a large extent the pace of agricultural development, but with maximal utilization of existing sources of water and with growing consumption for non-agricultural purposes, there will be changes made in the allocation of water. According to a forecast for the year 1980, the proportion of water consumption for agriculture will drop from 82 percent to 63 percent of total water use.

Electricity consumption is one of the main indications of the technological standard of agriculture and is an important factor in raising agricultural output, in addition to being one of the most important components in the standard of living and of culture in the village. The Israeli village is outstanding for its high consumption of electricity; in the year 1974 Israeli agriculture consumed 695 kw/h per hectare while other countries consumed considerably less. The data on other countries refer to the year 1960; USA, 61.1 kw/h per hectare; Austria, 73.5; Italy 20.5; West Germany 137.2.

In the last four years the consumption of electricity in Israel per hectare has risen by 39 percent (data from the Israel Electric Corporation, 1975). This signifies that there has been a considerable advance in the mechanization of the technological and agrotechnical processes in agriculture, that is, additional intensification of agriculture. The implication of this is of even greater significance; a technical infrastructure is being created in the village in the field of electricity, which also facilitates its servicing technological processes in non-farming branches in the village. In the period 1962-74, the consumption of electricity in Israeli agriculture rose from 78.9 million kw/h to 278 million k2/h, by 253 percent, whereas the cultivated area increased very little in those years (from 398,000 to 423,000 hectares).

Another important component of the techno-economic infrastructure is that of buildings, such as guest houses, industrial plants, farm buildings, public buildings, and offices. The following table shows the development in this field:

TABLE 9.7

Building for Economic Purposes in Town and Village in Israel,
1962-69
(by thousand square meters)

Year	Urban Settlements	Rural Settlements	Total	Rural Building as Percentage of Total Building
1962	938.5	360.9	1,299.4	27.8
1963	893.6	382.4	1,276.0	30.0
1964	1,102.8	526.2	1,629.0	32.3
1965	1,151.1	407.2	1,558.4	26.1
1967	583.0	469.0	1,050.0	44.6
1969	605.0	587.0	1,186.0	49.5

Sources: Building in Israel 1962-65, Central Bureau of Statistics, Jerusalem, 1966; and Construction in Israel 1967-1969, Central Bureau of Statistics, Jerusalem, 1970.

The above data demonstrate clearly that the proportion of building for economic purposes in the village is high compared to that in urban settlements.

Another very important component of the infrastructure in the village is transport, with the length of roads per 1,000 inhabitants serving as a standard of measurement of the roads network, while the number of vehicles per 1,000 inhabitants indicates the degree of motorization. The length of roads per 1,000 inhabitants in the Rural Regional Councils was twice as high as that of the urban councils (2.6 kilometers as compared to 1.3 kilometers) (Israel Statistical Yearbook, 1966, Central Bureau of Statistics, Jerusalem). The degree of motorization in the Israeli village in comparison with that of the town can be judged on the basis of the following table:

TABLE 9.8

Motor Vehicles According to Type of Settlement
and Type of Vehicle (1965, 1969 and 1973)

Type of Settlement	Vehicles per 1000 inhabitants					
	private cars			trucks		
	1965	1969	1973	1965	1969	1973
Urban settlements	31.9	50.5	76.8	14.5	19.9	25.6
Rural settlements	10.9	18.0	28.0	12.3	18.3	30.5

Source: Motor Vehicles, Central Bureau of Statistics, Jerusalem,
1966, 1969 and 1974.

The number of trucks per 1,000 inhabitants in the Israeli village
exceeded the urban standard in 1973. In the four years after 1969 there
was rapid development in this sphere, and the rate of growth in the
village was much faster than in town: the number of trucks per 1,000
inhabitants in town rose by 29 percent, while in the village it increased
by 68 percent.

THE PLACE OF AGRICULTURE
IN THE COMING TEN TO FIFTEEN YEARS

A forecast of the development of agriculture in the coming 10-15
years enables an estimate to be made of its place in the economy, in
terms of both employment and resources required, and of its contribution to the national product, In the year 1980, agriculture will
supply employment for 87,000 workers and in 1985 for 85,000 who
will constitute 6.6 percent in 1980 and 5.6 percent in 1985 of the
total number of persons employed in the national economy. Most of
the manpower in the village will earn a living in other branches of the
economy.

One of the considerations in the conception of the integration of
agriculture with other branches within the rural aggregate is to prevent depletion of rural settlements. However, in the light of the tendency apparent in the last 16 years—the decline in the place of the
rural population by about 30 percent, from 24.2 percent of the total
population in the year 1957 to some 17.0 percent in 1973—it should not
be assumed that it will be possible to curb this process completely, in
spite of the progress made in the development of industry and services
in the village.

It is more feasible to assume that development will bring about
a certain slowing down in the rate at which the proportion of the rural
population declines if the efforts and means used to enhance the integration process in the village are increased. It may be assumed that
around the year 1980 the rural population will constitute about 15 percent of the total population, and about 14 percent in the year 1985.

TABLE 9.9

Forecast of Number of Workers
in the Israeli Village for 1980 and 1985
(in thousands)

	1980	1985
Total Population	4,020	4,580
Proportion of rural population (percent)	15	14
Total rural population	603	641
Total work force in rural areas	212	224
Agricultural workers	87	85
Agricultural workers as percentage of total workers in rural areas	41	38

Source: Compiled by the author.

These figures indicate that in the year 1980 some 125,000 and
in 1985 about 139,000 village dwellers will require employment in
non-agricultural branches.

REGIONALIZATION OF PLANNING

The importance of the regional factor will increase in all the
agricultural changes forecast to take place in the future. Technological and economic development will bring greater acceleration in the
development of regional cooperation. Consequently, changes will have
to be made in the allocation of production factors. The criteria for the
allocation will be the optimization of the proceeds of every combination
of the components of production factors and every combination of
demand components. It may be assumed that, on the basis of the integration of non-agricultural branches in the rural areas, some of
the limitations that in the past existed to the optimization of agricultural production may be removed. Hypothetically, two main changes

are indicated: first, price policy—which in the past encouraged farmers of low comparative advantage to develop certain branches, thus acting against considerations of optimization—will now be based on broader considerations when they apply to a combined system of agriculture, industry, and services; and second, policies of production in the planning of agricultural production, which prevented the transfer of resources in accordance with comparative advantages, may be changed in a situation of production alternatives and broad employment opportunities.

Another aspect is the character of the interactions between economic activity in the village and that in the town with the advance in urbanization processes. A number of economists consider these interactions to be of prime importance. Thus, for example, T. Schultz went so far as to suggest that inequality in income from the agricultural economy is not the result of any difference in the size of the area of land or of the quality of the soil, but derives from the location of agricultural areas and their proximity to urban industrialization centers.[3] These interactions may be estimated with the aid of linear regression in order to create a correlation between the various agricultural components (such as areas of agricultural land, their financial value) and growing urbanization. In analyzing the correlation, expanding urbanization as an independent variable can be measured by the percentages of non-agricultural population within the limits of the urban municipal area. An analysis of this kind will be of assistance in reaching an evaluation of the extent to which urbanization will affect the different components of agricultural activity in the future. As to the past, the drop in the proportion of agricultural land in Israel should not be regarded as a factor which is seriously affecting agricultural development. The question is whether this rate of decline in the areas of land under agriculture will remain unchanged in the future.

The regional framework of integrated economic development will also require systems of integrative-regional analysis and follow-up. Schematically, it is possible to indicate the following components of this kind of analysis: the setting up of a logical-empirical system of regional economic integration which will constitute a macro-economic framework as a basis for the synthesis of the branch plans such as agriculture, industry, services, and tourism.

Various components will have to be elaborated as optimization models in accordance with the findings of the logical-empirical system and based on the requirements of the branch plans.

An alternative to overall development will have to be selected in accordance with the findings on optimization.

An analysis of this kind will enable a general conception of regionalization to be worked out which will take the following components

into account: population and labor potential, alternative patterns of
the economic structure of the region, the output of products and services within the region, reciprocal interaction between agricultural
and industrial development, input-output relations, and the regional
balance of resources and their use. The economic character of the
regional aggregate will be defined by integrating branch plans in such
proportions as will insure regional macro-economic optimization. An
analysis of the cash flows to and from the region is likely to show the
effect of the economic multiplier.

There is no doubt that regionalization of planning in the framework of overall aggregates will require a considerable change of
approach in macro-economic planning. This refers to the assumption
that not only those plans which are drawn up by the Agricultural
Planning Center will have to be aggregative regional ones; all government long-term plans and development budgets will also have to go
into detail on the regional level in order to insure coordination in
overall regional planning according to the following recommendations:

First, regionalization of economic development plans and government budgets. This will take the form of linking long-term development plans with clearly defined regions, with the state divided into
regions according to priorities. The boundaries of each region will
be specified according to geographic, economic, administrative, and
municipal criteria, and a long-term overall development plan will
be elaborated for it. In this framework of development strategy, the
development plan for each settlement will fit in with the overall
regional development plan.

Second, the development of the infrastructure. This is of great
importance for the consolidation of the regional aggregate, that is,
the coordination of the investments from government budgets in infrastructure—such as roads, electricity, and water—with regional development plans, the completion of a road network in order to strengthen
regional solidarity and to reinforce regional status of urban centers
in priority regions, the erection of central bus stations in regional
centers, and preference in developing the network of communications
should be encouraged.

Third, the consolidation of an integrated regional economic
system. This should include the following four components:

1. In agriculture and in settlement, emphasis is to be placed
on the encouragement of cooperation between agricultural settlements
(which are represented on regional councils) and urban centers, in
the sphere of regional development. Joint services as well as social
and cultural links are to be made available. Industrial areas and
centers of economic activity of the regional councils should be located
in the vicinity of urban-regional centers. In order to avoid a decline

in the population of the Moshavim, ways are to be sought to enable the
younger generation and other sections in the Moshav to engage also in
non-agricultural occupations. Preference will be given to agricultural
settlements in problematic areas by setting up projects suited to the
conditions of the regions with regard to hauling, inputs, and so on,
so as to strengthen the regional body while fully exploiting local advantages. The training of workers and vocational education are also
to be expanded.

2. The standard of building in priority areas is to be comparable to that in the center of the country and the settlers—young couples
of the younger generation in the existing settlements of these priority
areas will be given highly preferential assistance. In order to encourage the flow of professional manpower from the central parts of the
country to outlying areas, assistance will be given for the housing of
professionals in the fields of medicine, teaching, and cultural work.

3. In public services, there is to be an examination of the
feasibility of decentralizing higher education by means of building
colleges in priority areas to encourage equality of opportunity in
higher education for the youth there. Elementary and high schools
and vocational schools in those areas should be given priority in government budgets. The standard of health services in outlying areas should
also be brought up to that of the center of the country.

4. In personal services, the policy of allocating lands and
buildings for commercial and business services in the regions and in
the villages will serve as an important means of progress.

It should be stressed that these lines of policy are likely to be a
most important factor in the economic and social consolidation of the
rural aggregate which constitutes an important section of the regional
aggregate insofar as they will create a unified, integrated economic
system. This will also require institutional changes both on the nation-
wide level and on the overall regional level. Here it is intended to set
up legislative and administrative bodies such as a regional umbrella
organization to serve as the link between regional councils and local
and urban authorities. On the other hand, regional development will
necessitate the decentralization of government services and of national
public institutions. It will also lead to the necessity to draw most important institutional conclusions in the sphere of agricultural planning.
The transition from agricultural planning to the planning of the rural
aggregate will also require functional and institutional changes in the

direction of expanding the activities and authority of the Ministry of
Agriculture. If all the above developments are to be brought about,
it should become the Ministry of Agriculture and Rural Development. *

NOTES

1. "Urban-Rural Relations in Israel," Publications on Problems
of Regional Development no 8, (Rehovot, Israel: Settlement Study
Center, 1969).

2. "Spatial Organization of Rural Development," Publications
on Problems of Regional Development no. 3 (Rehovot, Israel: Settlement Study Center, 1968).

3. T. Schultz, "Expanding Urbanization and Selected Agricultural Elements," Land Economists, 43 (February 1967).

---

*These recommendations have been formulated by an inter-
ministerial committee.

10

THE INDUSTRIALIZATION
PROCESS IN THE
COOPERATIVE VILLAGE
IN ISRAEL
Arieh Szeskin

The modern cooperative movement has attained outstanding achievements in a limited number of economic branches, especially in agriculture and consumption. Attempts to expand the cooperative framework to industry and services have remained relatively limited in scope. Many difficulties were encountered in the expansion of co-operation in industrial production, where the movement came up against a broad range of obstacles which it has not yet succeeded in overcoming though efforts are continuously being made to find new ways of solving these problems.

It is generally accepted that the cooperative movement in industrial production can mainly succeed through enterprises set up by the cooperative consumers' movement. It would appear that there is an additional possibility of developing industry within the cooperative framework through the medium of rural cooperatives, especially in the light of the structural changes in the village which, to an ever increasing degree, has taken on the character of a diversified economic unit.

It is well known that Israel has succeeded in creating two original types of cooperative organization, the Kibbutz and the Moshav. Agricultural cooperation in Israel succeeded because the agricultural sector is suited to a cooperative system and because of the whole complex of ideological, economic, and social factors which characterized the Jewish community in Israel during the last hundred years. The economic revolution which is taking place in the rural sector throughout the whole world has obviously not bypassed Israel. Insofar as the cooperative system is concerned, this means that the very foundations of the cooperative organization have been undermined, and difficult problems have arisen in the sphere of relationships within the village itself. There are two important structural changes in the rural sector which have far-reaching effects on the future of agricultural cooperation. The first change is the modernization of agricultural production, a process which may be defined as the industrialization of agriculture. The characteristic lines of this process are increased mechanization, specialization, and larger production units, which inevitably lead to changes in the social structure such as adaptation to an urban way of life, with all its advantages and disadvantages, and to the creation of a stratified society. The other factor which has changed the social and agricultural structure of the village is connected with the penetration of the non-agricultural branches of industry and services, into the village.

We shall examine how the cooperative framework, which was from the outset adapted to the activities of the agricultural branch, has found new ways of adapting to different production processes and to new ways of life. We shall deal only with the cooperative aspect of the problem, and will attempt to examine the assumption that the cooperative framework can stand the test of change and find a suitable answer to the appearance of a new type of village, the ramified village based on a number of branches.

There are three main instances of the penetration of non-agricultural branches into the cooperative village in Israel, each with its own particular character and of differing significance insofar as the cooperative framework is concerned.

The first instance, connected with the development of Kibbutz industry is industrial enterprises, with all their specific characteristics of economic qualities (size of the enterprise, dependence on factors which are exogenous to the village) and their socio-organizational framework (the industrial hierarchy, specialization, and so on.

The second instance is the introduction of non-agricultural employment in the Moshav.

The third instance, which has developed at a rapid pace in recent years, is the regional enterprise, which is owned by the cooperative villages and which, while supplying a varied range of services to agriculture, also deals with industrial production.

INDUSTRY IN THE KIBBUTZ

In an examination of the industrialization process in the Kibbutz, the findings may have to be classified in two separate sections. On the one hand there is the quantitative economic balance, which puts the achievements of industrialization into their proper economic perspective. On the other hand, it is important to make a survey and an analysis of the causes which encouraged industrialization in the Kibbutz and of the problems and challenges which it raises in the Kibbutz society.

In the year 1973/74 the number of industrial plants in Kibbutzim reached 259, of which 80 new plants have been added in the last five years. In the last few years the rate of increase in the sales of the entire Kibbutz industry (in fixed prices) averaged 19 percent per annum. While sales reached 400,000,000 Israeli pounds in the year 1968/69, they exceeded the IL 1,700,000 mark in 1973/74. In the last year about 10,000 workers have been employed in these plants. The rapid rise in the pace of industry in the economic structure of the Kibbutz is remarkable. In a period of ten years (1958-69) the proportion of the labor input in industry out of the total labor input in the Kibbutz rose from 14 percent to 36 percent.[1] There was at least one industrial plant in each of about 80 percent of the Kibbutzim. The Kibbutz industry excels in its rapid increase of productivity, which was twice as high and more than the increased productivity in the same period in the entire Israeli industry. In addition to the productivity factor, Kibbutz industry is outstanding for its structure, which is based on concentrating on a relatively limited number of branches, as shown in Table 10.1. Some 66 percent of the total number of workers in Kibbutz industry are employed in three main branches: metals, wood and food.

As to size, Kibbutz industry is mainly based on enterprises which are considered large by Israeli standards. This is indicated by the data in Table 10.2.

The small size of the country makes it possible to set up industrial enterprises in rural areas which are nevertheless close to marketing and supply centers. The very fact of its being a "collective" has made a decisive contribution towards accelerating the process of industrialization in the Kibbutz. As a large production unit the Kibbutz was, from the outset, able to introduce industrial production processes and organization into the village. This is apparent in the high standard of agricultural technology in the Kibbutz, which is considered to be one of the most progressive not only in Israel but also in comparison with the most modern and highly developed agricultural farms in the world. It should be mentioned that the organizational forms of economic activity in the Kibbutz also helped to develop industrialization there. The multi-branched structure of the Kibbutz economy, in which every economic activity has its separate organizational and institutional structure, enables an industrial enterprise to operate within the existing economic framework.

TABLE 10. 1

Distribution of Workers in Kibbutz Industry
in the Year 1974/75
(forecast by branches)

Branches	Percent of Total Number of workers
Metal	31
Wood and furniture	17
Food	16
Electricity and electronics	6
Plastics and rubber	16
Textiles	3
Quarries	6
Chemistry	1
Miscellaneous	4
Total	100

Source: Annual Report 1973-1974 of the Association of Kibbutz
Industry, Kibbutz Shfaiim, June 1975.

TABLE 10. 2

Size of Plants in Kibbutz Industry and in
Overall Israeli Industry, 1973/74
(in percent)

Size	Plants	
	Kibbutz	Entire Industry*
Up to 10 workers	27	82
11-30 workers	32	11
31-50 workers	20	3
51-100 workers	14	2
Over 100 workers	7	2
Total	100	100

*The data on Entire Industry refers to 1972-1973.
Source: Annual Report 1973-1974 of the Association of Kibbutz
Industry, Kibbutz Shfaiim, June 1975.

Industrialization raised serious challenges for the Kibbutz movement, especially in the two following fields: the aspects of the principle of self-labor, and the socio-economic structure of the Kibbutz. There has been hired labor in Kibbutz industrial enterprises since they were first set up. There were periods when this problem was ignored, but recently it has caused heated discussions. According to the data for the year 1974, the number of hired workers in Kibbutz industry reached some 48 percent. Of 10,800 workers this year, only 5,650 were Kibbutz members. Sixty percent of all hired workers are employed in the ten largest plants, and it should be noted that the percentage of hired workers is especially high in the large old established branches (quarrying and building materials, wood and furniture, and food) whereas it is low in the newer branches (electricity and electronics, plastics and rubber). These data are given in Table 10.3.

There is also an economic problem, since the pay of a hired worker often costs the plant more than the working day of a Kibbutz member. Thus, hired labor not only affects the cooperative principles of the plant but also its economic basis. This is even more apparent when low output per worker is taken into account in a plant which employs hired workers, in comparison with a plant based on self-labor (member workers). Comparative data strengthen the assumption that the determination to avoid employing hired workers leads to greater efforts in efficiency, automation, technology, and various inventions, and in a reduction in the labor input.

TABLE 10.3

Proportion of Self-Labor in the Kibbutz Industry, 1974

Branch	Percent of Members Out of Total Number of Workers
Metal	56
Plastics and rubber	84
Electricity and electronics	80
Food	28
Textiles and leather	64
Quarries and building materials	27
Wood and furniture	26
Miscellaneous	95
Total Industry	52

Source: Annual Report 1973-1974 of the Association of Kibbutz Industry, Kibbutz Shfaiim, June 1975.

What are the possible solutions to this problem in Kibbutz industry? A number have been suggested, and some of them have even
been implemented, as for example, decreasing the number of workers
by replacing labor by capital (technological improvements); the setting
up of partnerships with other Kibbutzim, thus increasing the source of
manpower; partnership with a public body; and setting up cooperatives
of hired workers. Such experiments have already been in progress
for more than ten years, and indicate the many possibilities inherent
in the forms of cooperative organization for solving some of the
problems of industrial enterprises in Kibbutzim. An example is a
plant for the production of doors in Kibbutz Hamadia in the Beth Shean
Valley. This Kibbutz had produced doors at building sites but in 1963
decided to set up an industrial plant in the Kibbutz itself. This involved
the employment of about 40 workers and meant employing hired labor.
In order to avoid employing hired labor from the outset, it was decided to request the Cooperative Center to organize a cooperative of
workers from outside the Kibbutz who would be full partners in the
enterprise, with full rights and duties. The Kibbutz laid down two
basic conditions which were to serve as a basis for their agreement
to the setting up of a cooperative within the plant: first the plant was
to be set up in Hamadia, and second the Kibbutz was to have the con-
trolling vote in the company.

It was decided to set up a private company whose share capital
would be paid by both parties (the Kibbutz and the workers' cooperative)
according to the number of shares acquired by each partner. It was
also agreed that the workers of the company would be confined to members of both these bodies, and that members of the cooperative would
have to be residents of Beth Shean, in order to encourage the development of this small border town, which was in need of productive elements. In view of the fact that the members of the cooperative had no
means with which to finance the acquisition of the shares the Cooperative Center obtained special loans for this purpose, and the company
undertook to pay the cooperative ten percent of the monthly wage bill
for the repayment of this loan. Five members of the Kibbutz and two
of the workers' cooperative were elected to the board of the company.

It is interesting to trace the development of the wage system
which was introduced in this cooperative. It was decided to have a
uniform wage for all members. This arrangement worked well at
first, but when the company began to stabilize and the more highly
skilled workers became foremen or took on management positions, a
change took place in their approach to the question of salary. The fear
that these senior workers would leave the firm if this egalitarian wage
policy continued led to the decision that each member was to receive
his pay in accordance with his skills and his job in the firm.

Economically, the company attained considerable achievements. Following an arrangement whereby it was decided to divide part of the profits among the workers each month, and thanks to the introduction of a system of premiums and norms, the output was almost doubled within just one year—1970—and it may be assumed that this sharing of the profits played a considerable part in this increase.

On summing up the Hamadia experiment, one can draw a number of interesting conclusions. The Kibbutz solved the problem of hired labor in a positive way. A strong, if small, nucleus of 30 workers was formed which was committed to staying in the locality. The fact that the majority of the first workers are still employed in the firm speaks for itself. In addition, from the very outset there has always been a positive attitude to work in the plant. Some people believe that this is because of the existence of the cooperative, while others think that it is the result of the firm's efficient organization. It may be assumed that both these factors were contributory.

A number of difficulties that arose along with these achievements should not be overlooked. There is still no complete identification with the company, and members of the cooperative have not yet shaken off the mentality of hired laborers. The main management positions are still held by Kibbutz members. Nevertheless the Hamadia experiment appears to be most successful and holds great hopes for the future. Actually it still is a single experiment of limited dimensions, but some aspects of this experiment are of enormous importance. The very fact of setting up a partnership between two such different cooperative frameworks, both from the human as well as the structural points of view (an agricultural cooperative and an industrial cooperative) points to the great importance of expanding these new organizational patterns. Furthermore, the fact that a partnership was set up between a highly developed, technologically and socially advanced cooperative village with inhabitants of a development town indicates the possibilities of improving urban-rural relationships in Israel through partnership between the two systems, contrary to the existing situation in which the relationships between them, especially in the social sphere, are very tenuous.

Industrialization in the Kibbutz means a concentration of workers within the narrow framework of the plant, with the production processes increasing the ties and interdependence of the workers. This is significant with regard to the internal relationships which take the form of an administrative hierarchy and division of work. The relationships created in an industrial plant differ greatly from those in an agricultural enterprise. This problem of specific internal relationships in the industrial enterprise also raises many questions in the sphere of interbranch coordination within the Kibbutz. The problems raised here are both economic and social. From the economic aspect there is a growing awareness that the separation of the plant from the Kibbutz economy affects the principle of optimization in the allocation of production factors and in the scale of priorities in the development of the economy. It is thus understandable that there must be joint consideration with regard to the development of all the branches of the Kibbutz economy when determining financial planning, investments and a joint manpower plan. Socially speaking, it should not be forgotten that the Kibbutz is one socio-economic unit. Separate management for an industrial plant and for the agricultural branches and the services is liable to lead to severe damage to the social relationships within the Kibbutz and to create a stratified society.

Many researchers point out that the success of Kibbutz industrial enterprises is due in no small degree to the social suitability of the Kibbutz economy to absorb industry, as well as to its organizational advantages, the workers' identification with the enterprise, the fact that they are not seeking financial reward, the democratic organization of production, and the principle of rotation. There are certain dangers involved in Kibbutz industrial development though it is still too early to draw any final conclusions as to their extent. There are already a number of Kibbutzim where about two-thirds of the production workers are employed in industry without causing any essential change in the social structure of the Kibbutz, but occasionally it happens that the industrial enterprise constitutes a foreign body in the Kibbutz society, a completely independent unit beyond the interference of the economic and social bodies of the Kibbutz.

The essential problem is, therefore, the adaptation of Kibbutz principles and their application to the industrial enterprise. The success of the Kibbutz society is based without any doubt on coordination and identification of the economic and the social structure. Agriculture is based on relatively small branch teams, and in this way an egalitarian and democratic society is created in which a large number of people can identify with its structure and can be partners in making decisions. On the other hand, the structure in industry is in the form of a pyramid whose principles of management and technology impair the democracy and identification of the workers in the plant.

NON-AGRICULTURAL EMPLOYMENT IN THE MOSHAV

The problem of non-agricultural employment in the Moshav has raised serious difficulties from the very beginning. The Moshav, which operates its services within a cooperative framework while safeguarding individual production and consumption, is essentially based

on agriculture. The specific structure of the cooperative association
in the Moshav places agricultural activity at the center of Moshav life.

The basic difference between the Kibbutz and the Moshav in
this sphere is the far greater flexibility of the Kibbutz way of life,
which in turn is due to the fact that the Kibbutz is a large association
uniting within it both the economy and the society. This enables it to
adjust more easily to changing conditions. This fact obviously has
some implications when one examines the possibilities of industrializing the Moshav. Since it is based on small production units (family
farms) it lacks the economies of scale of the Kibbutz. Yet the Moshav
too has to find ways of adapting itself to diversified employment. While
the Kibbutz economy has succeeded in integrating the industrial enterprises within its socio-economic structure, with all the difficult
problems involved, for the Moshav the solution was to expand non-
agricultural employment for its members outside the Moshav. This
fact has very serious implications on the future of the Moshav, and
is the subject of stormy discussions within the movement itself.

The seriousness of the problems of working outside the Moshav
can be seen from the data of the agricultural census, held in Israel
in 1971:

TABLE 10.4

Employment Structure of Moshav Population
Aged 14 or Over in 1971

	Thousands	Percentage of Total
Full-time workers on farm	15.1	23.4
Part-time workers on farm	18.8	29.0
Working only outside farm	15.3	23.6
Studying, not working	15.7	24.0
Total	64.9	100.0

Source: Agricultural Census 1971, Preliminary Results,
Central Bureau of Statistics, Jerusalem, September 1972.

A considerable part of Moshav manpower is already working
outside the farm (23.6) and an even larger part is only partially employed on the farm (29 percent). This implies that in the present situation the family farm provides full-time work for only about 23 percent of the population ages 14 and over. Interesting data have been
received about Moshav members working outside their farms, as
shown in the following table (Table 10.5).

Employment outside the farm is characterized by a concentration of workers in the various services, especially the public services. In this employment structure agriculture takes a very limited place, and most of the workers outside their farms are employed in "urban branches." This does not mean that these jobs are necessarily in town, though in many cases that is the situation. Part of the services in which Moshav members are employed are located in Regional Service Centers, some of them in the Moshav itself. There is no doubt that as far as the Moshav is concerned, outside employment constitutes one of its most serious problems. Furthermore, as a result of growing employment outside the farm the principle of self-labor is also impaired. There is a growing tendency to replace self-labor in agriculture, where the remuneration is relatively small, with hired work, and at the same time to try to find more remunerative sources of employment outside the farm.

TABLE 10.5

Moshav Workers Outside Their Farms—by Economic
Branches, 1971
(in percent)

Branches	Moshavim (Ministry of Agriculture)*	Moshavim (Jewish Agency)*
Agriculture	15.0	19.6
Industry	10.5	13.8
Building	2.2	5.6
Commerce and finance	6.8	5.6
Transport and communications	6.6	5.4
Public services	51.0	42.1
Personal services	4.5	7.8
Unknown	3.4	0.1
Total	100.0	100.0

*The Division of Moshavim into the above two categories is due to the division in the assistance to agricultural settlements between the Ministry of Agriculture, which deals with economically consolidated settlements and the Jewish Agency, which deals with settlements which are in the process of stabilization.

Source: Agricultural Census 1971, Preliminary Results, Central Bureau of Statistics, Jerusalem, September 1972.

These facts illustrate the urgent need for finding a solution for the development of a multi-branched association within the Moshav

structure, and there are stormy debates going on among members of
the Moshav movement on this subject. There are people who, like
Hagai Benyamini, for example, claim that "insofar as industrialization of the village is concerned, there are two possibilities, the first,
that it be a cooperative in which all the members will share all the
profits—but then it will no longer be a Moshav. The second possibility
is that the members work in the association for pay—a possibility which
invalidates one of the main issues, the freedom of the individual to
create."[2]

There are others who, contrary to this approach, regard the
industrialization of the Moshav as inevitable. S. Assaf says, "There
are Moshavim today like those in the hills that cannot exist on agriculture alone and must find other sources of income. What is happening
to such Moshavim now? Outside work has replaced agriculture, with
most drastic social repercussions. Industry must be introduced, but
without destroying the values and social structure of the Moshav, and
this can be achieved only if the industry is owned by the Moshav, with
members of the Moshav enjoying both wages for their labor as well as
a share of the profits".[3]

Between these two extremist attitudes there is a growing awareness that ways and means must be sought to stabilize the cooperative
framework of the Moshav on the model of the ramified (multi-branched)
village. This takes the form of wishing on one hand to safeguard the
basic social values of the Moshav such as mutual assistance, while on
the other hand organizational and socio-economic changes are introduced into the structure of the Moshav association. This recognition
of the need for changes in the Moshav also arises from the fact that,
to a larger extent than in the Kibbutz, the Moshav faces the serious
problem of the younger generation. Obviously, if members of the
Moshav wish their children to remain on the farm they develop different branches and maintain a high standard of services, and none
of this is possible on agricultural activity alone. In other words, the
main problem facing the Moshav is how to safeguard cooperation and
mutual help in the process of specialization, technological development, and a rising standard of living.

In recent years there has been a clear tendency to seek ways of
industrializing the Moshav without affecting its cooperative structure.
While industrialization in the Kibbutz was the result of initiative "from
below," the cooperative association in the Moshav itself does not have
enough administrative and professional manpower or economic resources to initiate the establishment of an industrial enterprise. The
industrialization of the Moshav must, therefore, be implemented on
a broader basis than that of a single Moshav association. It has been
suggested that the industrial enterprises be located in a regional
center. Ownership must be in the hands of a regional association for

industrialization which belongs to the Moshav associations of the region in question. The suggested association will operate as a management company for the enterprises in its ownership, with partnerships with private capital and skills, and with the workers sharing in the ownership and management of each specific enterprise.

The suggested organizational framework for industrialization of the Moshav is based on three levels: first, the national level, which will deal with the organization of regional associations for industrialization, explore new projects, and so on; second, the regional level, within which Regional Associations for Industrialization will be set up; and third, the industrial enterprise itself, in which the workers and Moshav members will share in management and in profits. It has been suggested that the enterprise be organized as a shareholding company—and not as a cooperative association—so as to allow private capital to be involved.

THE REGIONAL ENTERPRISE— INDUSTRIALIZATION OF RURAL AREAS

We have hitherto discussed two forms of industrialization as carried out in the two main types of cooperative villages in Israel, the Kibbutz and the Moshav. There is a third type which holds great hopes for the advancement of rural areas, the regional enterprise. This type has the same purpose as the above two and has in addition, a number of important economic advantages. First, the regional enterprise creates broad opportunities for diversified employment. In the same way it contributes towards solving one of the most difficult problems of rural areas, the problem of emigration, especially of the younger generation. The creation of employment for a large number of professionals—accountants, clerks, engineers, technicians, plant managers, programmers, and various experts in production technology—gives new opportunities to trained young people. Yet another advantage achieved by the regional enterprises is savings in development costs and greater efficiency in the utilization of production factors by setting up industrial parks for a number of enterprises in one region. Efficiency in the utilization of production factors is achieved through increased manpower mobility within the regional enterprises and the settlements. Thus, for example, when the season of a particular crop comes to an end and the workers who were employed in sorting, packing, and similar jobs are out of work, they can be employed in other jobs within the industrial complex. The question of the direction which additional expansion should take is now confronting the regional enterprises. A long list of new enterprises which could be set up within the regional structure is being discussed. Among these plans the tendency toward vertical concentration of production in a particular branch deserves special mention. One example is the poultry meat branch in which the hatcheries, the slaughterhouses, and the plants for the processing of the meat can all be concentrated within the regional enterprise while leaving the actual poultry raising in the hands of the settlements which are partners in the regional enterprise. Suggestions have also been submitted for a concentration of enterprises to supply consumer services for the region. This development presents the cooperative village with new challenges. The question is, what are the limits of expansion of the regional enterprises and of transfer of functions of the single village to the regional body? Regional concentration matches the desire to take maximum advantage of economies of scale of the regional enterprises, but it also arouses concern in case excessive growth may lead to excessive dependence upon regional associations of the individual villages. This refers particularly to plans for establishing regional laundries, plants for the supply of prepared food to the dining halls of the settlements, and other consumer services.

The regional enterprises have now reached a certain turning point. The tendency to arrive at a clear division of work between the individual village and the regional enterprise is particularly apparent: the individual village is to deal with the various stages of raising agricultural produce, while the regional enterprise will handle all the other stages of production, both those preceding the raising of the produce itself (hatcheries for example) and the post-harvest stages (sorting, packing, processing, and so on). The regional enterprise can also serve as the focus for the supply of productive services such as equipment maintenance and, to some extent, can also supply consumer services.

On the ideological cooperative level the immediate question is obviously about the strength of the links between the regional enterprise and the cooperative movement. One of the outstanding points of the regional enterprises is the broad variety of organizational forms and institutional infrastructures. Though some of the plants are organized as shareholding companies and not as cooperative associations, the regional enterprise essentially remains an integral part of agricultural cooperation in the country. Two examples of the largest regional enterprises in the country illustrate this.

The first is Miluot near Nahariyah, with a large number of plants which have formed a most varied industrial combine which is rare not only in Israel but also in rural areas in other countries. This streamlined enterprise includes packing houses, a carding machine, a feed mixing plant, abbatoirs, a fruit processing factory, and other features, all of which are operated by most sophisticated modern methods. A special skill and development unit supplies research findings and recommendations for continuous development. Organizationally this enterprise operates as a limited company founded in 1960. The founding shares are divided as follows : 51 percent of the shares belong to the regional cooperative association which was founded in 1948, and the other 49 percent are held by the settlements themselves. In other words, though the enterprise is organized as a shareholding company the entire ownership is in the hands of cooperative associations. Incidentally, this form of organization is also widespread in other countries where the cooperative movement has set up industrial enterprises, as for example in the Scandinavian countries. The ordinary shares of Miluot are divided among settlements according to the volume of their production in the various branches. Apart from the enterprises entirely owned by Miluot, two affiliate companies have been established whose founding shares are all held by Miluot   (a fruit processing factory, Miluz, and a feed mixing plant, Milobar). Some IL 10,000,000 were invested in this enterprise in the year 1971/72.

Granot is another form of organization, it covers some 40 Kibbutzim in the coastal plain and is also considered to be one of the largest regional enterprises. Most of the production is carried out in a series of factories which still deal with primary handling of agricultural produce such as cold storage and packing of bananas and deciduous fruit, the storage of potatoes. Granot too has expansion programs which are in the stages of planning, such as the development of factories for the poultry branch.

Granot is organized as a cooperative association operating as the parent company, with four affiliate associations which are also organized as a cooperative association and which operate in various agricultural branches, such as a feed mixing plant, a cold storage plant and others. The parent company Granot holds 90 percent of the share capital of each of the four affiliate associations. The remaining ten percent belong directly to the member settlements. This method insures the central association of the control of each separate plant. The division of the profits is not uniform, but in the main takes into account the regular proceeds from the capital invested and the turnover of each member.

Though the regional enterprises are an integral part of the cooperative movement, the difficulties of safeguarding their cooperative character should not be overlooked. The main problem is that of hired labor which is even greater than in Kibbutz industry. Of some 4,000 workers employed in these plants, only 22 percent are Kibbutz members while the remaining workers are hired. In order to overcome this problem each member Kibbutz is obliged to allocate a fixed number of working days for the regional enterprise. There is obviously a

conflict between the interests of the Kibbutz and of the regional enterprise, and generally the interests of the settlement take priority,
especially when it applies to professional manpower.

Another problem is that of accepting Moshavim into a regional
enterprise that belongs to Kibbutzim. This question is not only ideological, but it involves many economic elements because the different
form of production organization in the Moshav differs from that of the
Kibbutz. While Kibbutz products are received in a uniform and organized
form, the large number of producers in the Moshav necessitates changes
and adaptation for their produce to be absorbed in the regional enterprise. Hitherto the regional enterprises belonging to Kibbutzim and
similar ones set up by Moshavim have remained separate. The beginnings of Moshav regional enterprises are most encouraging. Most
of the Moshav regional organizations are in the mountain region, where
prospects of agricultural development are relatively limited and alternative employment must be found.

From the cooperative point of view the regional enterprise can
be regarded as a higher level of cooperative organization, that is, as
secondary cooperation. The streamlining of a regional enterprise based
on cooperative foundations with the other cooperative settlements in
the region is likely to bring about completely new developments in the
cooperative movement. Regional integration on a cooperative basis
could be created, leading to the establishment of a "cooperative region"
which would include the whole rural sector and combine agricultural
with service and industrial branches.

NOTES

1. H. Barkai, "The Industrial Revolution in the Kibbutz,
Clarification and Comments," Research Paper no. 31 (Jerusalem:
M. Falk Institute for Economic Research in Israel, June 1972).

2. "Industrialization and Changes in Kibbutz and Moshav,"
summary of discussion held in Kibbutz Yehi 'am in March 1972
(Jerusalem: Settlement Department, Jewish Agency, November 1972).

3. G. Avni et al, "Streamlining Industry in the Moshav—An
Examination of Possibilities," (Tel Aviv: Ministry of Agriculture,
Planning Center, October 1972).

INDUSTRIALIZING RURAL AREAS: THE CASE OF THE ISRAELI MOSHAV
Yehuda Don

THE NEED FOR THE CREATION OF NON-FARMING EMPLOYMENT OPPORTUNITIES

The fundamental purpose of the Moshav movement at its genesis was the creation of a Jewish peasant, as a realization of the objectives of the renaissance of Jewish agriculture and nationhood in Israel. Massive expansion of the Moshav movement, during the first decade of Israel's statehood, made it into the strongest and quantitatively most dominant form of agricultural settlement organization. Expansion did not change ideological fundamentals, and agriculture remained the main occupation in the Moshav. Cooperative legislation has been based upon these facts. [1]

Recent developments have revealed the need for the creation of non-farming employment opportunities for Moshav members. There are three important aspects of this new development: first, the coming of age of the second generation in the post-1948 Moshavim; second, a radical change in the production methods in smallholders' farming; and third, the rapidly rising standard of living both in urban and rural Israel.

The vast majority of the 244 post-independence Moshavim—called "new Moshavim"—were founded during the early 1950s and were populated by families at the early stages of their childbearing life. From the late 1960s on the new generation, which grew up in the new Moshavim, have now become adults and have created a set of new problems.

An interesting differentiation in this respect is observable by dividing the new Moshavim according to countries of origin of their settlers.

TABLE 11.1

New Moshavim by Countries of Origin and
Average Family Size in 1972

Country of Origin	Number of Settlements	Average Family Size (parents included)
Asia and Africa	182	6.0
Europe, America, and Israel	40	3.5
Total	222	5.5

Source: Y. Don, R. Bar-El, Y. Greenshpan, B. Ilan, D. Shnitt, "Industrialization of the Moshav," research report to be published by the Settlement Study Center, Rehovot.

There is a very substantial difference both in the qualities and the dimensions of the second generation problem between the two subgroups.

The crucial issue for Moshavim of the second subgroup is how to safeguard intergenerational continuity. The small family and the educational ambitions of the founding generations toward their offspring regarding professional non-agricultural careers have greatly reduced the number of potential successors to the family units to be vacated by the aging founders. Consequently, in many such Moshavim the second generation problem has become one of persuading sons and sons-in-law to stay in the Moshav. The problem is twofold. On one hand, it is plainly quantitative, that is, how to prevent the desertion or permanent vacancy of retiring founders' units for lack of successors. On the other hand there is an acute qualitative issue, averting the dangers of qualitatively negative selection of those who do remain in the Moshavim. Thus, among the opinions on how to keep a sufficient number of the more capable sons and sons-in-law to stay in their Moshav, the idea of introducing technologically challenging non-agricultural occupations is gaining ground.

In the majority of the new Moshavim, those where the population originates in Asia and Africa, the second generation problem is totally different. Here the question is how to accommodate, physically, economically, and organizationally, every son who openly expresses his desire to live in the Moshav of his childhood. A survey conducted in a statistically reliable sample, revealed that well over two-thirds of all unmarried sons interrogated expressed their unreserved or partially conditioned desire to stay in their Moshav. [2]

Let us extrapolate the implications of the realization of such desire on the Moshav population for the next generation. First, 50 percent of all children are sons, secondly, sons are eligible for Moshav membership; third, two-thirds of all sons desire membership. On these assumptions, the expected net growth in the number of households for the next generation in a Moshav with 60 households at present will be twenty. In other words, an average growth ratio of 33 percent will be required to satisfy the desires of the second generation to establish their adult life in the Moshav in which they grew up.

The possibility for expansion of the Moshav's land reserves for future allocations is in most places virtually zero, and fragmentation of the existing holding is neither economically feasible nor is it permitted by the land tenure clauses under which Moshavim hold their land from the National Land Authorities. [3]Alternatively, massive investment in agriculture may drastically change capital-land ratios. Increasing capital inputs in the Moshav agriculture has been the policy of the planning authorities for some years. Results of such measures have been apparent in two directions. On the one hand, income per holding has risen remarkably, and the standard of living in most Moshavim has improved. In the new Moshavim this improvement has been particularly noticeable, and as a result income differentiation between the new and the old Moshav sectors has decreased considerably. On the other hand, however, capital investment in Moshav agriculture did not necessarily lead to an increase in the labor input. Very often it partially substituted for labor, thereby releasing the labor force for non-agricultural occupations.

In this respect it is useful to divide the new Moshavim into two distinct groups. First are the Moshavim situated in the lowlands, valleys, and plateaus, suitable for dairy farming and for intensive vegetable production. Second are the Moshavim in the hilly regions, where only deciduous fruit trees can be efficiently grown and poultry and eggs produced.

In the first category capital intensification has led to a sharp increase in average production per farming household and in employment in agriculture in those households. At the same time households which could not or did not want to expand production and which had in the past been pursuing part-time farming reduced their agricultural activity and increased their incomes from non-agricultural sources. Thus there is a tendency towards dichotomization in many dairy and vegetable farming Moshavim between full-time farmers and settlers who have ceased to pursue agriculture as a source of income and have thus become non-agricultural inhabitants of the Moshav.

In Moshavim of the second group, situated in hilly regions where agriculture is confined because of topographical conditions to poultry

farming and the growing of deciduous fruit trees, the course of development was entirely different. Capital intensification modernized production which, due to production quotas, was not allowed to grow
freely. As a result, instead of increasing production, the farmers
substituted capital for labor and released labor for non-agricultural
employment. Consequently, instead of the pattern of a dichotomized
valley we have a more or less homogeneous Moshav composed of
part-time farmers. The typical farmer cultivates his poultry farm
and orchard, usually with the help of his wife and children, and seeks
extra employment to supplement his income. This is demonstrated in
the following Table 11.2.

TABLE 11.2

Moshav Population by Non-Agricultural Employment,
Region, and Crop Patterns

| Moshav Pattern | Normative labor input (Number of days in a year) | | Farmers available for non-agri-cultural work (percent) | Farmers employed in non-agricultural work (percent) | $V=\frac{IV \times 100}{III}$ |
	I	II	III	IV	III
Topographic					
Hilly region	70	165	83.7	58.9	70.4
Other regions	152	262	55.5	44.8	80.8
Total	222	228	65.0	49.7	76.4
Agricultural					
Poultry	72	160	88.4	60.1	67.9
Dairy	61	243	51.6	44.8	86.8
Vegetable	89	283	53.8	43.4	80.7
Total	222	228	65.0	49.7	76.4

Source: Y. Don, R. Bar-El, Y. Greenshpan, B. Ilan, D. Shnitt, "Industrialization of the Moshav," research report to be published by the Settlement Study Center,
Rehovot.

Table 11.2 reveals that demand for family labor, calculated as
the product of physical production by regional labor norms for each

family unit and aggregated on the village level, * is on the average 37 percent less in the hilly areas than in other regions. The difference of about 16 percent between the average labor demand in dairy farming and in vegetable farming is not significant due to the steady, un-seasonal character of labor in the former as compared to the seasonal differences in the latter.

As a result of such a large difference in demand for family labor and the high interchangeability of family members' labor in poultry farming, 88.4 percent of all farmers in the poultry-orchard pattern Moshavim were normatively available for full-time employ-ment outside their family farms. Nevertheless, only about two-thirds of them actually did take up jobs to supplement income from farming, while the rest preferred extra leisure over extra income. †

In the other farming patterns the situation was different. Due to the dichotomized character of demand for family labor the heads of all agriculturally active farming units were, as a rule, fully employed on their own farms, while those who did not have full-time employ-ment at the farm had no employment at the farm at all and sought ex-ternal jobs. Well over 80 percent of all those normatively available for external employment were indeed employed outside their Moshav unit.

Higher capital intensity in the Moshav agriculture will not create additional employment opportunities for the second generation. In the poultry farming sector, where output quotas are effectively enforced, it releases labor which will join the second generation in seeking non-agricultural employment. In dairy and vegetable farming capital

---

*The formula used for the single Moshav was:

$$\frac{\sum_{j=1}^{n} 1_{dj}}{n} = \frac{\sum_{j=1}^{n} \sum_{i=1}^{m} q_{ij} 1_{i}}{n}$$

where 1_{dj} = demanded family labor in family unit (j); q_{ij} = production of product (i) in family unit (j); 1_{i} = standard labor requirement per unit of production of (i) in the relevant region. There are (m) branches and (n) family units in the Moshav.

†In 1972, when the survey was prepared "...unemployment was unprecedently low, and high rates of orders for labor were registered which could not be supplied." Bank of Israel, Annual Report for 1972 (Jerusalem: 1973): 192.

intensification increases capital/labor ratios and thereby causes higher labor productivity and brings about higher remuneration for labor in agriculture. Such a development is imperative to keep food production at an appropriate level under conditions of fast growing incomes in urban occupations. Capital intensification thus became a socio-economic imperative to avoid undesirable rural exodus and to ensure a reasonable level of agricultural output. It created, however, very little additional employment opportunities in Moshav agriculture.

INDUSTRIALIZATION OF THE MOSHAV

As indicated, recent demographic and economic developments have increased the potentially available labor force in the Moshav sector without increasing employment opportunities in agriculture. Such problems are common to many contemporary societies, and the customary solution is urbanization. In Israel, with its heavily urbanized social structure, * additional urbanization is considered undesirable. Among the prevalent policy measures aimed at avoiding further urbanization is the creation of non-agricultural employment opportunities for the rural population in the rural areas.

Two fundamental issues require careful examination in the course of considering appropriate selections of non-agricultural employment opportunities which may fit the socio-ideological-administrative context of the Moshav; the organizational or structural issue, and the issue of suitable production lines.

The organizational issue involves consideration of the specific conditions which emanate from the unique social structure of the Moshav. There are four main questions in this respect: the intergenerational conflict, the conflicts between farmers and non-farmers, problems of professional stratification, and conflicts between agricultural and industrial interests with regard to general resource allocation.

All these factors are capable of creating potential dissonances which may occur within the framework of intensive social and economic relations and may cause potentially hazardous frictions. The

---

*In 1971 only 10.5 percent of the Jewish population was defined by the Bureau of Statistics as "rural" and only 7.3 percent of all Jewish employed persons were "farmers and fishermen." Statistical Abstracts of Israel (Jerusalem: 1972): 31 and 320.

main decisions to be made in view of these issues concern location, scope, ownership, and organization.

Location. Industrial plants may be located within the boundaries of the Moshav, in a rural regional center, or in the industrial out-skirts of a nearby town.

Scope. The plant may aim at catering for the sub-Moshav level, as an enterprise of a number of members and/or sons from one or more Moshavim; or for the Moshav level, as an economic undertaking of the multi-purpose Moshav cooperative along with other agricultural or service enterprises; or for the inter-Moshav level, operating on behalf of a number of neighboring Moshavim.

Ownership. The plans may be owned by individual members of the Moshav(im); by one or more Moshav associations; by public, regional, or central authorities; or by private investors. There are of course possibilities for combined ownership.

Organization. Such an industrial plant may be organized as a private firm or a partnership, a joint stock company, a production cooperative, or a non-profit public enterprise.

This method leads to the elaboration of a profile system which theoretically includes all 144 permutations which arise from the listed contingencies. Consistent application of this method, after the elimi-nation of illogical or improbable combinations (such as private in-vestors organized as non-profit enterprise) leaves us with 47 profiles. The examination of the advantages and shortcomings of each of these 47 profiles in view of the distinctiveness of the Israeli Moshav reality should provide a rather clear idea of the organizational issues of Moshav industrialization. Interim results of an extensive empirical study of this issue have indicated that location in urban areas and the Moshav level scope may run into greater difficulties than, for instance, location in rural regional centers or both sub-Moshav and inter-Moshav scopes.

As regards the issues stemming from the production line selection, interim results indicate that chances for success are ex-pected to be relatively greater in industries with high interchange-ability of capital and labor; relatively low wage and work differentia-tion; unsophisticated and unstratified managerial systems; and pro-duction functions in which technical optimum is reached at relatively small scale.

Industrialization of rural areas has become an issue with fast-growing interest and immediate relevance in many parts of the world. The Kibbutz experiment, despite its remarkable success, is hardly applicable to different socio-economic contexts due to its extra-ordinary features. Extensive research towards a solution of the aforementioned problems in the industrialization of the Israeli Moshav may lead to converting it into a laboratory in the search for improved methods and techniques of rural industrialization in less-developed countries.

NOTES

1. A Schweitzer, "The Cooperative Settlements in Israel under the New Cooperative Bill," Yearbook of Agricultural Cooperation 1966, (Oxford: Basil Blackwell, 1966).

2. Y. Don, R. Bar-El, Y. Greenshpan, B. Ilan, D. Shnitt, "Industrialization of the Moshav," research report to be published by the Settlement Study Center, Rehovot.

3. J. Weitz, Land Ownership, Immigration and Settlement (Jerusalem: Jewish Agency, 1973).

12

NON-AGRICULTURAL
COOPERATIVE VILLAGES
Raanan Weitz

Rural cooperation in Israel, as elsewhere in the world, came about mainly in order to assist farmers to overcome difficulties encountered in their efforts to make the process of agricultural production more efficient. Rural cooperative communities are by their very nature "agricultural" cooperatives, which is to say that most of their members earn their livelihood mainly from agriculture. Up to the present, the division between agricultural cooperatives and non-agricultural cooperatives has been analogous to the distinction between rural and urban.

For reasons to be considered later in this chapter Israel is at present confronted with the need to promote the founding of rural cooperative communities, which are to be based on industry and on science-based services. This is the first social experiment of its kind. It presents a number of basic problems for both its initiators and for those who intend to carry it out in practice. This study is an attempt to describe the causes for such experiments and to offer an initial conceptual model for the foundation and development of communities of this novel type.

THE NEED FOR NON-CONVENTIONAL VILLAGES

The need to create a new type of village community has arisen recently in Israel due to two social factors, the absorption of the younger generation of farmers in rural areas, and the absorption of immigrants from affluent countries.

The structure of the Moshav limits the number of non-farming members in its community. The multi-purpose cooperative also takes on all the municipal functions of the village. There is complete identification between the committee that deals with agricultural affairs and the committee which deals with civic and municipal services. In order to maintain this identification the large majority of Moshavim in Israel have decided that the number of residents in a Moshav who do not draw their livelihood from agriculture and, consequently, have no direct economic interest in the cooperative should not be in excess of one-third of the farming population. Only one son of each farmer destined to take over his father's farm is eligible for membership in the cooperative. As a result of this decision the other members of the younger generation have difficulty in remaining in the Moshav and making their homes there despite the fact that it is their place of birth.

It is generally accepted that a large proportion of rural youth is destined not for agriculture, but for work in other occupations and for moving to various urban regions, where they can do this work. This corresponds to the assertion that occupational mobility goes together with geographic mobility. The number of farmers diminishes with the growth of efficiency in the process of production, and all those who cease to find their livelihood in agricultural production move either to neighboring towns or to more distant cities. This process, accepted as natural in most parts of the world, does not fit in with certain aspects of the structure of Rural Areas in Israel.

A large proportion of these areas has been settled by new immigrants from Oriental, African, and Asian countries who have carried with them a traditional patriarchal structure which they retain even after a quarter of a century in Israel. This is notable not only among the parents; it persists among the children educated in Israel. There is, therefore, a strong tendency in these villages to stay in the rural areas and to seek new opportunities there, even if they are not directly connected with agriculture. This tendency is seen in the establishment of non-farming enterprises, including industry, by farmers' associations in the rural areas. In the beginning the effort was directed mainly towards industry linked to agriculture and was either the kind which supplies agricultural inputs or that which processes farm produce. Lately, however, these associations have begun to engage in non-agricultural industries with the objective of creating non-farming employment in rural areas.

There are large areas in Israel where the development of agriculture is difficult or even impossible due to their mountainous or desert character. This makes it impossible to set up a network of

villages sufficiently dense to maintain civic, cultural, and economic
services, at a reasonable level. The settlement of such areas can only
be carried out if a way is found of setting up villages whose income is
based on non-agricultural employment.

ABSORPTION OF IMMIGRANTS
FROM AFFLUENT COUNTRIES

The absorption of immigrants from advanced countries (from the
affluent countries of the Western world as well as the U.S.S.R.) has
necessitated a search for the formation of new social units. The absorption of such immigrants has lately been accompanied by increasing
difficulties. Signs of dissatisfaction, failure to adjust, and even difficulties in relating to the realities of Israel society have been widely
manifest. The author of this chapter has made attempts to study the
sources of these difficulties, to analyze their causes, and to determine the fundamental factors involved. The two principal factors seem
to be the problems of social absorption and the lack of a challenge for
these groups of immigrants, by which they could express their direct
involvement in the process of national development.

SOCIAL ABSORPTION

The mass immigration which took place in the early 1950s
taught us the fundamental lesson that the head-on collision of different
ways of life arising from different cultures impedes successful absorption. When an individual or a family is confronted with a culture
alien to them, the chances of overcoming absorption difficulties are
minimal. Social absorption in heterogeneous groups has proved to be
very unsuccessful. The problem is even more serious today than it
was in the days of mass immigration. We are not dealing now with
two different civilizations, one of which is inferior to the other, as
we were in those days. At present, it is people who belong to cultures
in many ways competitive with Israeli culture who have to be integrated.
The danger of a confrontation between competitive cultures is much
more serious than any we have previously known.

The kind of social absorption that is reasonable, healthy, and
appropriate to the goals set by Israeli society for its newcomers can
only be achieved where conditions allow the immigrants to integrate
through their own efforts. In other words, social absorption is

practical and accessible, not to individuals or isolated families, but only to entire communities conducting their daily existence in accordance with their own way of life.

THE NEED FOR A CHALLENGE

Israel has been built up by successive waves of immigration. Each of these waves has made its specific contribution to the country and has had its special national social challenge. Today the situation is rather different. The arrival of immigrants is accompanied by absorption programs which allow them to be welded into the existing social structure and to fill in gaps without any clear, specific challenge for them. It is a serious mistake to think that the immigrant arriving in Israel nowadays seeks only to get there, and nothing more. There are many immigrants in search of a challenge, be it in the social, developmental, or settlement field. The problem is that we have not found a way of defining these challenges and of presenting them clearly to the immigrants.

Non-agricultural cooperative villages could constitute such a challenge. Settlements of this type can be populated with communities which are homogeneous as regards their culture, their way of living, and even their occupations. They comprise a social challenge of the highest degree if employed in creating socially valuable cells of a new type of community organization. They can prove suited to the educational and professional background of immigrants from advanced countries, whose training and educational background can find adequate outlet in forms of employment with which they are familiar and experienced from their countries of origin. If implemented, the proposal outlined here may result in the creation of communities based on a set of special values without precluding the utilization of modern technological and scientific advantages.

A MODEL FOR NON-CONVENTIONAL RURAL COOPERATIVE COMMUNITIES

The structure of these proposed settlements is based on three main points: first, they will be run according to the rules of a cooperative community. Second, they will constitute closed communities, entry into which will be dependent upon acceptance by an elected committee of the settlements. Third, the size of the settlements will be limited. They are to be large enough to form an independent community which can maintain adequate services but sufficiently small to prevent their turning into towns. The size can vary between 150 and 300 families according to regional requirements, the character of the inhabitants, and the kind of occupations envisaged for each settlement.

KIND OF COOPERATION

A specific kind of internal organization is needed to form an intermediate link between the conventional urban organization and the cooperative association of the Moshav. One suggestion is that the settlements under consideration should be administered by a committee elected by all the members. The committee would be responsible for social, cultural, and municipal functions, but would also operate as a kind of apex organization for economic activities. Economic enterprises could function separately, owned and managed by the members they employ. The apex organization would help with the planning of these enterprises and deal with their common problems such as finance, technical and legal consultation, purchasing of supplies, and marketing. All enterprises thus developed would have to belong to the apex organization. The auditing would also be supervised by this organization.

KIND OF ENTERPRISES

The choice of industrial enterprises to provide adequate employment to the settlers must take three factors into account. First, the choice of enterprises must suit not only the members of these non-agricultural settlements, but also those of the existing rural settlements in the region. Second, the scope of the enterprises must ensure economies of scale in the present and future. Third, attention must be given to the level of education, professional training, and personal inclinations of the candidates for this type of settlement in the selection of enterprises.

THE ORGANIZATIONAL FRAMEWORK
AND SOURCES FOR INVESTMENTS

The organizational framework and the financial means needed for the establishment of settlements of this kind demand a specific approach. We must bear in mind that opportunities should be left open to the private initiative of these settlers in accordance with their professional skills, while at the same time guarding against misuse of public monies or land belonging to the community. In this connection the following scheme seems pertinent:

1. The land, allocated to each settlement, is to be registered under the name of the cooperative community and not under that of individual members. Members are to have the right to sign a lease only after they have repaid all the public capital invested, or after they have provided adequate financial securities.

2. Investment in housing will be forthcoming in accordance with the conditions for settlement practiced in this country. Anything beyond these limits will have to be borne by loans to the apex organization on the financial conditions generally accorded to development projects.

3. Financing of enterprises is to be implemented in accordance with accepted practice in the establishment of "approved" enterprises.

4. In certain regions the development of special agricultural branches might be taken into consideration, in conjunction with industrial enterprises and services (for example, poultry, hothouses, and fresh flowers).

PROSPECTIVE MEMBERS AMONG IMMIGRANTS

The selection of candidates for membership of such settlements would be in accordance with the methods tested and developed by the Settlement Department of the Jewish Agency in the establishment of cooperative agricultural settlements. These non-conventional settlements ought to be affiliated with a "settlement movement," as are most of the settlements in Israel. Enlistment of prospective members from abroad ought to be carried out, as far as possible, in their countries of origin.

PROSPECTIVE MEMBERS FROM AMONG THE YOUNGER
GENERATION IN ISRAELI VILLAGES

The organization of candidates for settlements of this type must
be undertaken by a special unit of the Settlement Authority. Its function will be to direct them to occupational training and to organize
them in groups for the establishment of such settlements. To this end,
the cooperation of the various settlement movements should be sought.

All these suggestions are only indications of the direction to be
taken. Life itself is the best guide in social experiments of this kind,
as we know from our experience with the Kibbutz, the Moshav Shitufi,
and the Moshav Ovdim. There are three necessary conditions for
success: First, the active support of all institutions dealing with
settlements of this type. These institutions must be made aware of the
value and importance of the undertaking and must have a realistic
notion of the difficulties to be overcome in the process. Second, the
voluntary organization of the candidates, whether it consists of the
younger generation or of new immigrants. Volunteering should be
based on a clear picture of the social units to be set up and on the
assumption that the effort is worthwhile even if it involves a change
in one's way of life. Third, encouragement from the Israeli public
in general and from the settlement and political movements in particular. This will be necessary to foster an atmosphere supportive of
social experiments of such innovating character.

THE ORGANIZATION FOR IMPLEMENTATION

The process of founding settlements of this new type is complex.
Since it affects every avenue of human activity, it comes within the
orbit of all governmental ministries. Ministries are structured on
vertical lines, each tending to act on its own, with staff and line in-
structions moving from the highest level down to the field workers.
Interministry coordination can therefore be achieved at the national
level but is very problematical at lower levels.

The process of settlement and development involves the interests
of individuals, families, and communities, and requires the full cooperation of all public bodies concerned with actual implementation in
the field. The integration of new immigrants into rural regions in
Israel has been successful for a variety of reasons, not least of which
is the existence of a body which coordinates all activities on the site
of settlement. In contrast to the usual structure of ministries, this

authority is structured on horizontal lines, undertaking the planning, implementation, and coordination of all that concerns the development of the rural community at the regional and local level. The structure and tradition on which this development authority (The Settlement Department of the Jewish Agency) is built is most suited to deal with the kind of novel social units envisaged here. It is sometimes argued that the proposed settlements do not correspond to rural villages but instead constitute urban elements and should, accordingly, be dealt with by one of the ministries responsible for urban development. This argument is unfounded, for conception of setting up village complexes based on industry and services is aimed at improving rural status in modern society and adding to it a new dimension which answers the needs of our time. Non-agricultural cooperative villages can be a milestone on the way to creating valuable social units appropriate to our scientific and technological era. They constitute a challenge which affluent western society cannot afford to overlook.

THE FIRST REALIZATION OF THE IDEA

There are three kinds of non-agricultural cooperative villages presently in existence.

The Nevei Ilan group consists mainly of members of the Yehuda Hatsair youth movement active in the United States. The first members of this group arrived in Israel in 1969. The founding group consisted of 56 families. There were a number of drop-outs and reinforcements. The group consists at present of 40 families. By the final phase of settlement the group ought to comprise about 80 families. Most of the families have already moved into permanent housing in Nevei Ilan.

The enterprises envisaged are to correspond to the qualifications of the members, most of whom have academic training in the natural sciences, social sciences and the fine arts. Thus, projects proposed include industrial plants, services, and consultancies. Already in operation is a plant for the manufacture of electronic appliances, a computer service and consultation center, and art courses for schools. In addition a recreation center including a school for hoteliers, a motel, and a sports center is being planned. Finally, an agricultural branch, turkey breeding, will augment the industries and services.

The Aliyah 70 group is composed of immigrants from the Soviet Union, mainly from Kiev. They are all academicians, for the main part engineers, who arrived in the country after 1970. The group consists of 20 members who have formed a limited liability company.

In order to strengthen its potential and diversify its range of activities the group is on the lookout for new, non-academic members who can be absorbed into projected enterprises. Training courses to prepare some of the members for the types of industries projected, are also being programmed. These are electronic and optical industries and chemical laboratories.

Yahdav (Kfar Etzion C.) is a group composed of 25 young religious families from the United States. The heads of these families are in the process of completing M. A. s or doctorates. They include electronic engineers, programmers, chemists, psychologists, and the like. Some of the wives are teachers. Other groups, similarly qualified, will be added to this group. In consideration of the qualifications of the members, industrial and chemical plants and a boarding-school for maladjusted children are among the projects planned. This group will be located in the Etzion region, where the settlement programs are ready for the first phase of implementation.

13

THE STRATIFICATION
SYSTEM OF THE KIBBUTZ
Eliezer Ben-Raphael

PRIMARY STRATIFICATION

In light of the sociological model of "exchange"[1] social reality
can be approached as an interminable system of interconnected roles
through which people make contact with the object of obtaining valued
commodities, material or otherwise. There exists in society a continuous stream of notable objects which may be acquired by various
ways and means. It is customary, according to Weber's classic distinction,[2] to classify these factors in three main groups: those with
a common denominator which indicates a relationship of esteem, honor,
or prestige conferring privileges on resources; those connected with
power, coercion, or deterrence, which may all be reduced to the
concept of strength; those which regulate the flow of material or economic goods whose exchange value is a direct consequence of the exchange of objects, such as money, which is in itself a symbol of
material goods.

In the primary group, the most restricted of social set-ups, with
its face-to-face relationships, mutual appreciation is one of the main
factors making for distinctions between its members from the stand-
point of their place in the group (that is, social status). Moreover,
the higher the latter rate this appreciation, the more they tend to conform, in this way reinforcing conventions and norms of behavior.
Thus no stratification map is ever uncomplicated, no matter how
small the group to which it relates is. However, on account of the
primary nature of the relationships, each member has a defined
status with regard to all the others which arises from his distinctive
capabilities and behavior, but it is doubtful if this appreciation alone
creates wide gaps in small groups.

Where the group is bound to a common objective, entailing at least a minimal division of labor among the members, some of them take responsibility for supervision and direction with regard to the others. These would be the same members who enjoy the special appreciation of the majority. But in as far as the common objective is more complicated and requires specific skills, experience and special training grow in importance. These qualities, on which the group is dependent, are liable to constitute sources of power in the hands of individuals.

Generally speaking, the infiltration of power into the primary group multiplies the possibilities of the formation of status distinctions, expressed in growing formalization of the mutual relations between the various levels. As opposed to this, the relations between status equals (as employed in the term "strata") are freer, even though this interaction is of less consequence in terms of reinforcement of personal status.

It is against this background that the problem of status imbalance becomes comprehensible. It brings about a reduction of reciprocal activities and an increase of isolation within the collective. Another source of the weakening of the intensity of social relations lies in the number of members. In sociological and psychological literature[3] it is emphasized that the forms of social relations grow geometrically where the number of members grows arithmetically. It follows that there is no possibility of face-to-face contact beyond a certain number of members, though a social framework in which so many needs are provided that social contacts remain primary can be envisaged. Accordingly, in addition to the number of members, a total view of the scope of the life of the society is essential in classifying a collective as a primary or secondary group. So long as the member is obliged to maintain direct contact in the diversified relations with the majority of the members of the group, the latter remains primary. As a result, no decisive formalization of status criteria comes into account here.[4] The stratification principles observed in a collective of this type are presented in this paper under the term primary stratification, namely, a stratification system possessing clear properties which develops in the primary community and which includes most of the social behavior of its members.

In a collective of this type it is not only that the intimacy in social relations diminishes on account of the lower intensity of mutual relations but that the principles of stratification grow progressively more complicated. The gaps between the bottom and the top of the scale widen, and the horizontal interaction gains greater significance and symbolizes the status level of each individual and his place in the collective. As a consequence of this the stress on strata identity grows and is liable to act as a focus for any struggle regarding the definition of the status system. In other words, there already begin to appear in the primary group which has reached a sufficient size, stratification processes that culminate in the consolidation of subgroup identities. As a result the question of status imbalance receives a further dimension: when the members of the group differ on principles of justice, the general consent to individual status decreases, and with it also the personal security of the individual about his status. This situation does not of course strengthen the cohesion and the feeling of belonging in the group.

Nonetheless it is not to be concluded from this that the fate of every large primary group is to fall apart and fragment into new groups, a possibility which is only one of many. Social problems involving breakdowns affect not only the privileged but all the other members as well, so that integrated steps taken within the group to prevent the emergence of conflicts, disagreements, or a sense of alienation, may be expected.

STRATIFICATION IN THE KIBBUTZ

Leadership—Groups and Strata

The concept of a primary group of broad dimensions is appropriate to the reality of the Kibbutz. While some Kibbutzim count their members in tens, there are others whose numbers run into the hundreds and even thousands. Most of the settlements number between 250-400 members, and between 500-800 persons. *

The Kibbutz has been described as fundamentally a model form of development for the nation as a whole. The extremism of the new behavior patterns required within this framework turned intensive ideological identification into a prerequisite for membership, from the very beginning, every course of deviation being considered heresy. The institutionalized arrangements were represented as being the only possible way of realizing aspired values. [5] Patterns, accepted

---

*250 to 400 includes men and women (18 years of age, and over) as members, whether married or not. The difference between this and the latter estimation accounts for the children (under 18) who become members after reaching the age of 18, and after their service in the army.

through force of necessity in specific conditions, were absorbed into
the ideological picture, so that, originally part of the realistic
characteristics of the Kibbutz, they turned into components of an
ideal type.

At this stage the status differences were not acutely felt, and
the main distinction made was between those "belonging" to the collective in the full sense of the word and those who did not as yet enjoy
that standing. But even then there emerged, at times prior to the
actual settlement on the land, social leaders who earned their position
through their ability to give systematic expression to the practical
implications of pioneering ideology, and to offer themselves as a
personal model of symbolic significance. Identification with these
leaders was considerable means of achieving identification with the
collective that they represented and consolidated.

At the same time, the creation of settlement in the framework
of an autonomous enterprise produced not a Marxist utopia, but a
form of organization more reminiscent of Proudhon's conception, as
is apparent from the official designation of every Kibbutz, namely,
"a collective settlement of a workers' group." What developed was
not an entire society rejecting private ownership of means of production, as perceived by Marx, but rather an autonomous social cell with
its own private resources. Economic orientation and the harnessing
of effort for the increase of profit did not disappear, but became the
concern of the collective group. This is the reason that economic
rationalization[6] was adopted and an instrumental leadership developed
which specialized in the coordination and supervision of effort and
investment.

Despite all this, the social values to which all conformed were
not rejected, nor did they lose their dominant importance, so that
the new instrumental leadership could not gain any prime footing
without taking after the ideological values. Rivalry between the social
and economic elite became possible, without any direct dependence
between the two. This situation did not necessarily create serious
conflict. The ideological conformities basically require devotion, as
well, to the economic problems of the collective. Opposition is liable
to break out over more secondary problems, especially with regard
to the relative valuation of the various activities (remunerative or
productive work, as opposed to educational and cultural services,
and the like).

In the first phase the existence of power, generally speaking,
made itself felt in such things as organizational ability, capacity for
leadership, general education, and familiarity with the field of agricultural work. These were the qualities which singled out the economic
elite. Wherever competition between this economic elite and the social

leadership emerged, even in minor matters, the importance of the general meetings of the membership or of the Kibbutz' informal discussion sessions as a means of settling differences of opinion increased. This was the peak period in the history of these institutions, when a choice between alternative approaches, economic or ideological, had to be made. [7]

In the following phase, a decrease took place in the position of this supreme institution of the Kibbutz. In the wake of the development of various institutionalized spheres toward greater specialization, industrial production engineers, agronomists, educational psychologists, trained economists, accountants, and efficiency experts began to emerge. Consequently general meetings delegated a large part of their former functions to committees and sub-committees which partly operated on a professional, more than on an ideological basis. As a result the informal Kibbutz discussion session was, in many cases, transformed into a meeting of no more than symbolic or expressive importance.

The tendency to status imbalance began to grow in this phase, general approval in a certain field not necessarily implying positive attitudes to the personality as a whole. Thus, members were able to entertain contradictory valuations with regard to the standing of other members involved in different branches of activity, (for example, educationists as opposed to farmers). Under such circumstances factors familiar to us from the sphere of social psychology are liable to come into serious operation. [8] Thus, after years of specialization and the concentration of effort in a specific direction, a sense of disappointment can ensue, and expectations can be transferred to other spheres.

It is with this for a background that a change can take place in the relative significance of two kinds of rewards. The more ramified the Kibbutz' social system becomes, the less is the power position of members of any standing measured against the diffuse assessment arising from conformist behavior. This represents a decrease in esteem, primacy of the regard for conformity, as far as ideology is concerned at least. Further, insofar as status is dependent on competence of the kind obtainable in institutes for higher learning, an acknowledgment of status is created with regard to the extra-Kibbutz system as well, with the result that the dependence of the individual on the Kibbutz as a whole decreases.

To all intents and purposes, there is an interaction between the processes which encourage expertise and specialist training for the various undertakings and those which conserve the places of the social leaders. While such processes consolidate the extent of stratification of the Kibbutz, the latter remains an unmistakable

primary group despite the widening of its scope. The extent of stratification is embodied in the concept of strata and is reflected in the
fact that a great part of the relations between Kibbutz members occur
on a homogenic status level.

In the past the Kibbutz underwent stratified heterogeneity as a
result of the advent of groups of pioneers who created various social
circles. [9] These circles occupied a more or less uniform place as
regards elements that affect status, such as seniority, age, working
experience, or cultural integration. There were, of course, themes
about which the circles differed, such as the attitude to activities
in the Kibbutz movement, or in youth organizations. There was sometimes even open contention about the different standpoints supported
by each side (as in various spheres of work, public roles, cultural
or educational activities, and the like). A few Kibbutzim disintegrated
as a result of conflicts of this kind. This happened in cases where
there was a failure on the part of veteran members to effect the social
absorption of new groups, or where differences of opinion regarding
ideology caused disruption. As a result, the absorption process considered most successful is one where the ascriptive bonds (for example, land of birth, age, or original pioneering movement) of the
social groups were in the process of disappearing, and mixed groups
were crystallizing around the leaders of public opinion, and other
central figures. Even at the present time all kinds of circles still
exist, though they are far from including all the members of the
Kibbutz. Actually, as a result of the processes described above
(factors contributing to the spread of status imbalance and to the lack
of public uniformity with regard to the individual standing of each
member) there is noticeable on the part of many members a tendency
to minimize their social contacts on account of the fact that they find
them frustrating and even depressing. The resultant withdrawal into
the bosom of the family leads to further contraction in general social
life. [10]

For years now the Kibbutz has been undergoing a process in
which the family has been growing in strength as against other frameworks such as circles of friends, work friendships, or connections
with members of the same origin. This is for many reasons a most
distressing symptom. In the early days the position of the family in
the Kibbutz was of the most abject since the collective put itself in
its place. [11] But even at a later period the right of man and wife to
membership, independently of each other, was strongly upheld. Very
strong educational systems were set up and the education of the
children was defined as a collective responsibility. As a result of
these approaches, it was to be expected that certain of the functions
filled by the family in modern society would be effaced. Yet despite

the fact that the Kibbutz has made a successful bid to get even with
the technological and economic objectives of our time, and despite a
structure intended to reduce the place of the family, the latter has
reached a point of strength much greater than that which pertains in
extra-Kibbutz society.

A functional sociological explanation is that development follows
on a process of increasing specialization in various institutional
spheres. The family, as every other sphere, develops distinctive
orientations which foster its specific functions. So too, a broader
basis for family development has grown, giving the family an almost
exclusive monopoly of the affective orientations in Kibbutz life. This
has resulted from the rationalization of all undertakings, and the ex-
punging of any emotionally expressive elements from their limits.

The increased strength of the family can also be attributed
in part to the contradiction existing between the principle of equality
of the sexes officially upheld in the Kibbutz and the inferior status
actually accorded to women in the employment set-up. The latter
constitutes the principal component in the definition of the individual
stratification position. She is pushed into such jobs by virtue of external customs and values which oblige the woman to undertake the
kind of work where she is supposed to be more "efficient" than men.
In this way she is denied most of the productive positions which are
most esteemed in a society living on the marketing of its agricultural
and industrial products. Thus the family acts not only as a compen-
sating factor but also as a mechanism whereby woman's status is
reinforced. As mother of a family the female member is no longer
looked upon as just employed in "consumer" or "service" occupations
by Kibbutz agencies, the various managers, or general membership.
At all events, the efforts of the women of the Kibbutz to fortify the
family are unconcealed. The latter goes from strength to strength
annexing important items which previously belonged in other institutional spheres (for example, consumption allowances which have become familial instead of individual, or the fact that children spend
more and more time in afternoons and evenings with their parents
instead of in the children houses). In addition to all this, the family
stands out as a factor towards liberalization, insofar as it offers
defense against the infiltration of the collective establishment into
the more private areas of life.

This process has reached such significant proportions that it
has become publicly recognized as legitimate. In a veteran Kibbutz
family groups sometimes number dozens of individuals (including
several generations and various family branches and their ramifications) who retain a certain solidarity. It is hardly surprising that
even if the social and economic situation of the Kibbutz is not of the

best, the individual member does not lack a sense of home, on account of the constantly enlarging scope of the family.[12] This development is made possible on account of the rural ecological background of the Kibbutz. But there is no doubt that its main source is in the much deeper problems of the collective which adopts radical communal patterns.

One of the conclusions to which these social developments lead is that a social interaction is generated which is, in part, not open to control. Thus with all the status differences between members of the extended family their behavioral relations are characterized by a staunch solidarity. Furthermore, those members who maintain social relations in the main with their status equals are less subjected to a general normative orientation. However, this may be, the significance of this dilution of central control in the Kibbutz which remains primary despite its growth is that there is an accumulation of tension between points of relationship, stratification criteria, and even between various value approaches. This tension intensifies as the gaps between the status levels in the society, which views equality among its most esteemed values, grow.

The Ascriptive Factor

Various explanations are offered for the fact that status differences are often also accompanied by differences in work satisfactions. Thus the lot of a director of an industrial enterprise is different to that of the member whose place is by a machine in the same factory. It is also true that people working outside the Kibbutz do enjoy many benefits not available to those who remain at work in the fields. As a result of this there is a tendency to reformulate the value of equality: it is considered still valid so long as the advantages acquired by certain members can be demonstrated as appropriate to the function they fulfill, and so long as these specific advantages do not invest them with privileges in any wider sense. Both these points refer in the main to the sphere of consumption which is characterized in the Kibbutz as in any modern society by the basic existence of scarcity. Consumption is the aspect most emphasized, comprising as it does the declared objective of the immense effort invested in production. Under such conditions of relative but continual scarcity, the materialization of equality becomes complicated.

The Kibbutz solution to the problem lies in a combination of the universalistic approach and the ascriptive orientation: whatever part of consumption goods is not divided on a basis of content equality

(each one being provided according to his needs, as in the case of
nutrition) or on a classified basis (each being paid the same sum of
money, as in the case of clothing budgets) is linked with ascriptive
properties which eventually apply to all (for example, according to
age or seniority). It is in accordance with this that the members are
classified in various groups which are eligible in turn for the various
products (refrigerators, better housing, improved furnishings, and
the like). A certain amount of inequality becomes legitimate on this
basis. It does, however, require that there should be agreement about
factors like age or seniority becoming the basis of consumption demands. Thus the ascriptive factor infiltrates into the Kibbutz as a
policy by which the groups competing for products are to be recognized.
But just as the various status dimensions overlap at times (age and
seniority being mainly connected with working experience, hence to a
certain extent to status), so are these groups liable to struggle too,
over supervisory or other public roles.

There also exist in the Kibbutz other elements which are conducive to value significance being given to socially ascriptive groups.
The group of founding members is, for example, accorded especially
high regard in comparison to other veteran groups who do not date
back to the very beginnings. Moreover, as in any revolution striving
for social stability, the Kibbutz places a charismatic value on its
successive generation, the ideological fidelity of which is proof of the
success of the founders having created a permanent form of life. As
a result, the younger generation of Kibbutz members enjoys a not
inconsiderable number of extra privileges. Thus the Kibbutz opposition to studies, considered non-essential as regards the immediate
necessities of the community, folded in the face of demands on the
part of the younger members for university education. Similarly,
new and costly patterns of consumption, such as foreign travel were
accepted. These are only a few out of many examples testifying to
the special consideration accorded to the younger members. Actually
another explanation for this phenomenon lies in the fact that the younger
members are the first to be able to rely on forceful support of parents
who are themselves veteran members of the Kibbutz.

There are also more alternatives open to a Kibbutz-born member starting out in life: having completed secondary school, there is
nothing against his taking up professional studies. This enables him
if necessary to acquire a status on the outside no less respected than
that which awaits him inside the Kibbutz. For this reason the younger
member has strong bargaining power (having recourse to open or con-
cealed threats to come to his own conclusion), in event of his wishing
to demand concessions. Other members equipped with special qualities
have at times access to this kind of power too, but in every instance
its employment entails a downgrading of social valuation.

Elitism of the Kibbutz

In fact it was not inner development alone that gave rise to the importance of the ascriptive factor. From the very start the Kibbutz took a stance as a status group in regard to society at large; in asserting that it fulfilled the highest values of society and the nation, it took upon itself the task of being the main focus of values, involving responsibility of a nature extending beyond its own self-interest. The strong connection between the Kibbutz movement and education, whether in the Yishuv (Jewish population) of the pre and post-State period, or in the Zionist movement in the Diaspora, goes back to this. In actual fact, it was this value-definition set up by the Kibbutz which paved the way for its deep involvement in the higher spheres of the political system. The latter, on account of its revolutionary Zionist character, required a legitimate basis for the new social order to be established. Settlement on the land with its emphasis on universal values constituted a strong sub-structure in consolidating a legitimization of this kind. [13] Of equal influence on the standing of the Kibbutz was its readiness and capacity to take on tasks of public importance, such as those connected with security, immigrant absorption, or the general economy of the country.

The prestige and political standing that this gave the Kibbutz was reflected in all its members. The mere fact of belonging to the movement invested the whole community of members with the prestige and respect accorded to a specially placed group, to such an extent that their leaders found themselves part of the national political elite.

It was this powerful standing that in the course of time was to some extent responsible for a sharp decline in their position. [14] This took place as a result of demands made to be accessory to the central decision-making councils after the fashion of "political vanguardism." The consequent splits within the Kibbutz movement and isolation of most of the Kibbutz movements from the main political powers lasted some time and led to its banishment, so to speak, to the outer fringes of society. Their part in carrying out idealistic, symbolic, educational and particularly tasks to do with settlement, did not however, entirely disappear.

A further reason is to be found in a change in values which took place in Israeli society after mass immigration and the failure of the Kibbutzim to prove effective in the area of immigrant absorption. There took place a partial transfer of the function of settling to other types of settlement while at the same time the security importance of civilian concentrations on the borders was reduced, as a result of the establishment of proper army defense forces. The Kibbutz was

affected more than anything else by the processes of institutionalization which appeared on the political front, stressing the statehood
symbols of the political system. As a result of this, the areas initiated
and manipulated directly by the state machinery were more favorably
placed while the value approach to independent sectors began to weaken.
There was also an increase in the relative importance of new status
groups, such as economic investors and entrepreneurs (private as
well as public), academics, and high-ranking army officers. This
came about in the wake of increased technological development in the
economic sphere and the continuation of the serious security situation. [15]

The main consequence of all this is to be seen in the undermining of the position of the Kibbutz in the social system generally,
and in the extreme shift in the correlation of rewards of the Kibbutz
member. These two factors are inextricably linked. With the decline
in his status the Kibbutz member turns to his own institutions with
demands in the direction of consumption and privacy that are compen-
satory. This encroachment on the impregnability of various institutional arrangements weakens the ideological identity of the Kibbutz
and necessitates the reformulation of definitions. The latter finds
expression in a system of formal regulations which has as its object
the stabilization of major aspects of this way of life. These regulations must be confirmed by the Israeli Parliament through the application of special legislation. Steps such as these are taken at the expense
of the high-minded revolutionary dedication of the Kibbutz society in
relation to its external environment to such an extent that the Kibbutz
is rated as an organic part of the latter instead of an alternative to it.

Parallel with this adaptation come attempts on the part of the
Kibbutz movement to renew its status, such as are evidenced in its
readiness to release younger members for prolonged army service
in select units. In this way it reserves for itself a unique standing in
the Israel Defence Army (Zahal). There is also the projected Kibbutz
university which has been in the offing for years now. One of its aims
is to create a direct link between higher education, on which increasing
value is being placed by Israeli society, and between the Kibbutz movement as such. Similarly, regional Kibbutz enterprise has received a
strong position in the economic and industrial sphere. This effort has
invested the Kibbutz movement with a significant position as one of
the new economic groups of Israel, the industrial entrepreneurs. [16]

With all these different measures under way, new possibilities
open up before the Kibbutz, both as regards the establishment of a
prominent standing and of increasing its strength, effecting increased
cooperation between the various Kibbutz organizations.

The basic difference between the situation presently crystallizing and that which existed previously is that there is no longer

so direct a connection between the system of Kibbutz values and the
standing of the movement in society. Nowadays there is more need of
tactics and strategy, though it is doubtful if the latter are always
clearly defined and consistent enough to gain any additional advantages.

SUMMARY: PERMANENCE AND VARIATION
IN KIBBUTZ SOCIETY

The foregoing remarks illustrate the great difference between
the "modern Kibbutz" and that of the past. Recognizable traits have,
nonetheless, been retained so that the term Kibbutz is generally still
of special sociological significance today.

In the beginning, in the golden era of pioneering (1904-24) the
external environment of the Kibbutz was composed of scattered groups
of workers very much resembling those who took part in cooperative
settlement. The Kibbutz was at that time very small in size, consisting
mainly of still unmarried idealists. They formed a kind of sect in which
the functional leaders wielded more influence than others on account
of their organizational capacity though the style of life accorded
greater importance to the ideologically expressive leadership. The
basic orientation of the Kvutzot and the Kibbutzim of those days was
towards the personal fulfillment of utopia.

With the great strides made in the general progress of the
country[17] in the early thirties, Kibbutz society also reached its peak.
External conditions were then subject to strong influence of the working
class sector, which also held a central position in the World Zionist
Organization. The political establishment stood for a collective approach, so that the Kibbutz, fulfilling official values of this very kind,
was accorded high status as a result. It became the central focus for
widespread youth movements which acted as reservoirs of manpower
and took an intensive part in political life. In those days concern over
ideology was strong and was carried in a ramified movement mechanism. At the institutional level the uniformity of the original sect turned
into a complicated system of specially organized structures, economic,
educational, and ideological-political in character. As a result, the
stratification aspect also became more diversified with the spread of
authority over a wider area. The functional leadership on the one
hand, and the political movement and social activists on the other,
comprised the dominant elements, each characterized by a diffuse
approach and by far-reaching ability. There emerged, out of the
strong social, ideological, and value position of the Kibbutz, a strong
sense of pioneer vanguardism which easily developed response to the

demand for an all-encompassing leadership. The more these demands
were satisfied, the more the gap between the general political organization and the Kibbutz movement grew. It is here that we find the
fundamental background for the splits in the workers' movement.

Today the external environment of the Kibbutz is primarily made
up of a polity of institutional systems with values and characteristics
that are widespread nationally. The symbolic value position of the
Kibbutz has been only partially retained principally in the symbolic
settlement connection (population of frontier areas that makes the
frontier legitimate). Simultaneously, Kibbutz society has reached its
highest peak as far as its internal situation is concerned: from the
"sect" of the early days it has turned into a multi-generation community with extended families deeply rooted in its midst. Together
with more formalism in socialization and values, the Kibbutz developed successfully as a veritable home for its offspring Further
differentiation then took place, leaving its mark on the composition
of the primary stratification system. It is this that explains the
growth of the social power factor and the shift in the standard of
mutual esteem among the members. Social strata started emerging,
so that ascriptive struggles troubled this society too in the wake of
an increase in the consumption function. These circumstances, on
the other hand, are characteristic of the basic orientation of the
Kibbutz towards the rest of Israeli society. This represents a desire
to fit into the general institutional and legal establishment with the
object of using the advantages at its disposal in realizing the fundamentally elitist aspirations prevalent.

There are important factors which have stayed fixed and stable
throughout. First and foremost among these is the negative attitude
to money as a factor of stratification. Up till now concepts such as
wages, shares, or similar considerations have not come into account
as a means of differential individual remuneration for participation
in production. Consequently the positive extremist approach of developing autonomous collective resources has persisted, which is to
say that the settlement supplies the basic economic necessities and
calls for clearly defined efforts. Moreover the fact of its being a
primary group with face-to-face relationships explains the importance
of its informal social controls—the social system is ultimately based
on a self-image which allows the Kibbutz significant social functions
in society as a whole. These properties form an essential part of any
definition of the Kibbutz society.

But, to be considered as well is the fact that the social changes
following on the growing distinction made between the various institutional spheres and the proliferation of the stratification system are
also far-reaching. These processes led to a large degree of formali-

zation in the relationships pertaining between members, which increased with the institutionalization of the Kibbutz social order and
its inclusion in statutes and legislative clauses. This clarification of
the basic attributes of the Kibbutz comprises a change in the system
of collective concepts, on the one hand, and a limitation of collective
authority over themes connected with the individual, on the other.
Consequently, fundamental liberalization in connection with the promotion of the freedom of the individual at the expense of the common
lot and essential equality, is accompanied by formalization. Further,
there develops on the part of the individual members an attitude to
the collective, from intensely ideological to functional and perhaps
even instrumental. This is also true to a certain extent as regards
the attitude of the Kibbutz to potential roles that it may take on in the
wider society.

The future of the Kibbutz depends to a great extent on the extent
of interactions between the two categories of factors described above:
those showing great permanence, and those which show visible change;
or, in other words, between basic values and institutionalized principles. This interaction takes place at three levels which together form
a kind of circle: the first level is in the relation between the sociological reality of the Kibbutz and the demands of its value-system,
the second in the basic distance between that and the values prevalent
in Israeli society, and the third in the actual interaction with the external environment. The first point is inextricably bound to problems
of Kibbutz stratification while the second relates to the stratification
position of the Kibbutz in the Israeli social system. It is the dialectic
between these two which gives rise to the third.

In an effort at abstraction, this study on the factors which
cause change in the Kibbutz social system can be made to relate to
the levels at which these changes take place. It then becomes abun-
dantly clear that the special dynamics to be seen in the development
of the Kibbutz are linked to the deeply problematic interactions between the fundamental value system of Kibbutz society and the primary
stratification reality. The disparity that exists between them acts as
a lever in the continual search for patterns of adaptation to the
problems which arise as a result of this same disparity.

NOTES

1. G. C. Homans, The Social Behaviour: Its Elementary Forms
(New York: Harcourt, 1961); S.N. Eisenstadt, "Continuity and Change
in Stratification Systems," in Meganot 19, no. 1, in Hebrew.
2. Bendix, Max Weber, An Intellectual Portrait (New York:
Anchor Books, 1962), pp. 285-328.
3. W.R. Scott (ed.), Social Processes and Social Structures
(New York: Holt, Rinehart & Winston Inc., 1967), pp. 214-15.
4. W.A. Faunce, M.J. Smucker, "Industrialization and Community Status Structure," American Social Revue 31: 390-99.
5. Sepher Boussel - Tarbout Vehinouch (in Hebrew) pp. 234-35;
237-39 (Heb.).
6. E. Cohen (ed), "Changes in the Social Structure of Work in
Kibbutz" in Eisenstadt, Social Structure of Israel (in Hebrew) (Jerusalem: Accademon, 1966), pp. 436-51.
7. J. Peres, "The General Meeting," Avnaim no 3 : pp.
76-107, in Hebrew.
8. Homans, op. cit.
9. Y. Talmon, Garber. "Social Differentiation Within Kibbutz,"
Individual and Society in Kibbutz. (In Hebrew) (Jerusalem: Magnes,
1970), pp. 205-22 (Heb.).
10. E. Ben Rafael, V. Kraus, Y. Taglacozzo Leaving the
Kibbutz, in Hebrew (Haifa: Haifa University, 1974).
11. Y. Talmon - Garber. "The Family in the Kibbutz," Garber,
op. cit., pp. 12-36.
12. "The Family and the Roles of the Second Generation."
ibid, pp. 146-70.
13. S.N. Eisenstadt, The Israeli Society, (Jerusalem: Magnes,
1967), pp. 130-33.
14. M. Braslowsky, "Workers Movements in Eretz Israel,"
Kibbutz Ham'oo'had Tel Aviv (1952).
15. M. Lissak, "Image of Society and Stratification in the Jewish
Society of Eretz Israel and in the State of Israel," ed. Eisenstadt,
op. cit., pp. 203-14.
16. Y. Talmon, Garber, E. Cohen. "Collective Settlements
in the Negev." op. cit., pp. 264-301.
17. S.N. Eisenstadt, The Israeli Society, op. cit., pp. 10-28.

14

**THE DANGER OF INDUSTRIAL
SUCCESS TO THE KIBBUTZ—
DISCOURAGING OBSERVATIONS OF
A NON-PROFESSIONAL SPECTATOR**
Avraham Yassour

Is the Kibbutz going through an industrial revolution, or is the industrial revolution bypassing the Kibbutz? What are the social implications of industrial expansion on Kibbutzim?

Industrial revolution is a controversial term. Even though I accept Marx's analysis of the industrial process as shown in Capital, nowadays the process is different in developing countries, especially in particular sectors like the Kibbutz movement. However, one may note certain apparently common characteristics: information on production methods leading to a higher level of general education and greater rationalization of social relations; abolition of traditional forms and development of new relations in production; an accelerated rate of capital investment; changes in the division of labor, and social disjunction.

Other consequences reported by different researchers—for example, population mobility, breaking up of the family structure, changes in ownership forms and productivity—do not make themselves felt in the Kibbutz in the manner in which they were described. This does not mean that they lack relevance to industrialization of the Kibbutz, but that they appear in quite different forms due to the social structure of the Kibbutz and its notable successes in "agricultural industrialization."

It seems that H. Barkai was correct in his lecture at the Van Leer Institute (1972), when he stated that the industrialization process of the Kibbutz should not be termed an industrial revolution. Yet certain social and ideological changes may be identified which are linked to industrialization or at least were speeded up somewhat by it.

The industrial process taking place in the Kibbutzim is remarkably successful and rapid, and has resulted in the establishment of some 200 very modern industrial plants in a period of 10-15 years. Their financial turnover has become a determinant factor in the economic life of the Kibbutzim in four ways. First, the financing of industrialization has derived only in part from sources within the Kibbutz itself. Second, Agricultural employment is in a constant decline while there is a continual increase in the employment of hired workers and the number of persons employed in industry has practically quintupled. Third, the share of agricultural production and income from agriculture in the total production and income of the Kibbutz movement is in a constant decline. Fourth, there has been a steep rise in the living standards of industrialized Kibbutzim, and they therefore serve as models for less developed Kibbutzim; create a sharp imbalance between Kibbutzim (a new phenomenon which already causes concern to the leadership of the Kibbutz movement—I. Ben-Aharon* has also commented on this problem; and become increasingly dependent on the prospering of a single and dominant production branch.

But, as we have already pointed out, our interest centers only on the consequences of the process and not on its adequate description. More specifically, we are concerned with ordinary known consequences of the industrialization process in capitalist societies, although the Kibbutz is considered an alternative to these societies. Thus this review leads to a comparative study of such consequences. We would undoubtedly be interested in a comparison with the Societ Union's extraordinary industrialization realized at the same time as its collectivization of agriculture, its absorption of financial means from internal reserves, but conditions are so different that they defy comparison.

The industrialization of the Kibbutz emphasizes the crucial question of the amount of manpower employed in a single production branch and its share in the total income of the Kibbutz and of the changes which arose in the priorities for the division of labor, in the forms of management and decision making, in the concept of autonomy for a single production branch in the totality of the Kibbutz economy, in the rotation of senior leadership functions, and in the prestige attached to work in the different branches. Above all, we must ask ourselves whether the Kibbutz society still uses the direct democratic processes in all its decisions, processes which have assured the identification of the Kibbutz member with his work.

We certainly do not belittle the extraordinary results obtained by the Kibbutz industry, some of which are flattering for the movement:

---

*Former Secretary General of the Histadrut (General Federation of Labor in Israel).

the worker, well-educated, skilled in mechanized cooperative-collectivist agriculture, shows an outstanding adaptability in moving from agriculture to industry. The Kibbutz, with its many branches of activity, has succeeded in providing excellent manpower and in raising capital for the development of its industrial enterprises. Through industrialization, the varied needs of the population in different age groups can be satisfied, and great mobility for the adult population becomes possible.

Nevertheless, one cannot ignore the fact that in a decade, half the manpower of some Kibbutzim has been absorbed by industry. This became possible because the above mobility was operative. However, we have reached the limit of possibilities; there is no solution but that of continually increasing the employment of hired workers. The country's affluence has encouraged the investment of capital, but it is not difficult to visualize an end to this process in the future. The market for industrial products may experience stiffening competition, a handicap that agriculture has not encountered because of cooperative marketing and its adaptation to the needs of the country. Prosperity has a certain effect on the internal relationships within the Kibbutz and a crisis (or local failure) may well lead to the collapse of the Kibbutz, which leans towards a monoculture. In the near future the problem will become more evident: is Kibbutz industry really different from the capitalist industrial process? That is to say, won't the laws of competition apply and result in an internal concentration, a monopolization of the market, the spawning of a bureaucratic hierarchy, and a depersonalization and uprooting of the worker, even if he is the owner?

It has been demonstrated that in the industrial Kibbutz enterprise, the percentage of hired workers depends on the size of the factory. An increase in the number of hired workers furthers the process of formal hierarchization. The rarity of change in jobs, due to the limitation of mobility and to specialization, accentuates the tendency toward bureaucracy. The identification of Kibbutz members and factory workers with the factory and its needs decreases. It becomes necessary to offer material incentives such as the use of cars, and travel abroad.

To this process is added the striving for greater profits as a goal which can be achieved under chaotic market conditions through adaptation to a more radical competition. From there on the inequality between Kibbutzim becomes more marked, and the central authority of the movements diminishes. It is unlikely that Kibbutzim can live with this situation for long. In many Kibbutzim the paradoxical question is: will the industrial enterprise be one of the economic branches of the Kibbutz, or will the Kibbutz be a village dependent on the factory?

There is no "back-to-nature," even though the phenomena described here are not factors of the technological nature of industry.
The great challenge of the Kibbutz to be industrialized and to remain
a Kibbutz is still to be met.

The Kibbutz has successfully developed a collective and mechanized agriculture due to its very characteristics as a Kibbutz. The
development of agriculture was identical to the process of productivi-
zation so evident during the return to the homeland, to the pioneer
process of national renaissance adopted as the collective goal of the
groups of settlers. On the contrary, the industrialization process
of the Kibbutz started at a time of weakness, a time when the Kibbutz
movement was characterized by an ever-increasing identification of
the Kibbutz with its capitalist environment (the number of second
generation members leaving the Kibbutz indicated the extent of the
process): when individualism dictated a civilization of consumption
and pleasure masquerading as "self-realization," when economic development was becoming a goal in its own right at the expense of
human values. One does not have to be a pessimist to draw the conclusion that the entrepreneurs in the Kibbutz, pioneers of industrialization, are very rapidly becoming a pressure group, with all its
negative attributes.

The more the members of the Kibbutzim take advantage of the
fruits of economic prosperity, the greater the dangers. They are
therefore interested in stability and efficiency, the systematization
and rationalization of the capitalist spirit (almost within the terms
of Weber's "Protestant Ethos") leading to similar tendencies in all
aspects of life and spirit, the "mercantile fetishism" becoming a
dominant factor accompanied by a levelling through statutes. Homo
economicus brings the spirit of capitalism inside the socialist framework. If a "de-economization" of the Kibbutz members is not carried
out as rapidly as possible, it is unlikely that the "vessel's" shell
will support this new load.

Such processes can be detected in various spheres:

First, in the Kibbutz meeting. This is the loftiest expression of
direct democracy: it cannot work properly as long as the decision-
making processes are not uniform for all the branches and all the
members, as long as the "expert" carries more weight as far as
opinions and decisions are concerned, as long as an ordinary bureaucracy engaged in a speeded-up development of industry is not opposed
by the force of genuine self-management, as long as industrial successes increase the advantages of the individuals without causing
them to be conscious of the quality of collective life.

The meeting thus becomes a means for transmitting tendentious
information and ceases to be an effective framework for the processes

of direct democratic decision-making in communal and egalitarian
life. The process of formal institutionalization and the increased importance of the "experts" will finally lead to the formation of a hierarchical pyramid with the elite of status at the top.

Second, in education. The rationalization of personal relations
brought about by industrialization (and in reality the formalization of
the relations, linked to the attainment of "middle-class respectability,"
which increases inequality) has resulted in neglect of the individual
needs of the young students and in a greater demand for technical
professionals. Kibbutz education, based on general needs and abilities,
has been replaced by a specialized differentiation, a selection accelerated by the formalization of its results in order to attain status. The
crisis of the Kibbutz educational system has lowered the prestige of
educators, "service employees" who can be hired cheaply from outside the Kibbutz. The idea of "transfer of goals" is well known and is
denounced as detrimental to the future development of the Kibbutz. The
technical specialists refuse to be "items" on the duty roster, and
finally cannot understand why they must live in the Kibbutz of all places.

Third, in comprehensive budgets. Allotment of comprehensive
standard budgets has been suggested for the use of each member of
the Kibbutz in order to develop individualism. Certainly this yearning
for individualism (which is termed "personal realization" and may
contain an attractive bit of non-conformism) constitutes a safeguard
against a bureaucracy advocating a mechanical equality in the satis-
faction of the individual's needs. But under present conditions it
seems to lead to more inequality and promotes centrifugal tendencies
in various areas. Thus it would cause more paradoxes than the structure of relations existing in the Kibbutz is able to cope with (such as
the needs of artists, scientists, and external workers).

Fourth (and most serious) in the fate of equality. Equality cannot exist in the formal climate of a society subjected to the manipula-
tions of external and internal capitalist influences. Kibbutz society
was constituted when rebels joined together against their environment (pioneers and utopians, with social and national goals). A new
society based on what L. Mumford calls "mad rationality," where
economic efficiency is the dominant factor, cannot exist. To a certain
extent this contradicts the spontaneous dynamics of industrialization:
in order to survive, the Kibbutz must subordinate its industrial development to its organic development.

The Kibbutz is based on an ideological decision which has
generated the will to live a communal and egalitarian life. There is
no higher aspiration than to be what you are in conditions you your-
self have created according to your own criteria (within the realm of
reality). The criterion of investment of capital under Kibbutz conditions

can be based not on economic-quantitative usefulness, but on social-qualitative usefulness, which actually means less expansion and more equality. Doubts have been raised about the future of the Kibbutz movement when the younger generation takes over from the founders. It was assumed that increased consumption will reinforce the framework. But considering rising consumption as a goal is only a step away from conspicuous consumption, which feeds on the inequality of material compensation. The expectation of compensation leads to the awarding of compensation. However, to consider material compensation as an incentive leads to increasing contradictions in the Kibbutz. Whether these contradictions are useful or not, they are dangerous to equality and self-management, which have proven very effective in the development of cooperative agriculture. The same danger is present in an increase in the number of hired workers.

Since we have acquired so many extraordinary things in our Kibbutz life, it seems today that efficiency means slavery to external goals. This is why we have formulated the following suggestions: reduction to the absolute minimum of institutionalized authorities; expansion of their Kibbutz responsibility; total abolition of any budding hierarchy through a constant and complete turnover of responsibility; self-management of equal members united by their independence without excessive advantages to technical specialists (without detracting from their prestige); and renewal of professional and general humanist education (in the spirit of Fourier, Marx, and Gordon) as part of the effort for renewal of the socialist ethos centered on man and his needs instead of on the acquisition and fetishism of capitalist consumption, which in the end reinforce private ownership and a lack of equality. Without equality there is no free and mutually dependent society.

Classic industrialization has led to the summit of the capitalist ethos; the process of industrialization under Kibbutz conditions leads to a confrontation between the capitalist ethos and the socialist ethos in its actual implementation. When the possibility of success has been proven, one still faces the following question: Will (in Martin Buber's words) "utopia which has not failed" continue under the conditions of a prosperous industry?

15

**INTER-KIBBUTZ
COOPERATION IN INDUSTRY**
Abraham Daniel

The concept of inter–Kibbutz cooperation in Israel developed gradually and had great impact on the rural areas. It started with improvization, which later made way for planned operations. This cooperation was in the main the outcome of the social aspirations of the settlers and of their desire to make their farms more efficient, to organize their marketing and the acquisition of the means of production, and to create additional employment and increase productivity.

This form of cooperation emerged even before 1948. With the establishment of the state, social and economic changes took place in rural settlement in general and in the Kibbutz movement in particular, leading to the creation of patterns of cooperation between Kibbutzim.

MOTIVES FOR COOPERATION

There are two motives for the creation of such patterns of cooperation, economic and social.

Economic Motives

1. The setting up of large scale enterprises in order to decrease costs (economies of scale).

2. The rapid technological development of Israeli agriculture and the widespread introduction of industrial crops (such as cotton, sugar beet, and ground nuts) which compelled the farmers to acquire expensive and diverse equipment.

3. The need to mobilize high level professional manpower as a result of the large scope of the enterprise. Increased production in the various branches as a result of greater know-how required different tools from those previously used by Kibbutz members and increased the impetus to introduce scientifically-based modern technological methods.

4. The need for large scale capital investment in equipment and in various other production factors, which no single Kibbutz could carry alone, and the need to exploit the various capital investments to the full in order to achieve profitability.

5. The necessity to meet the requirements of the market, competition in the urban markets, and surpluses in various production branches and their effect on prices. The increased standard of living and the demand for quality products demanded flexibility and adjustment. These could only be obtained efficiently by inter-Kibbutz organization.

6. The need to create sources of non-agricultural employment, both in order to augment the income and to absorb excess manpower.

Social Motives

1. The need to absorb the younger generation and encourage it to remain in the Kibbutz.

2. The need to prevent negative social effects which are likely to arise as a result of an unemployed marginal population.

3. The wish to give the young people higher education in order to prevent the gap that is liable to be created on the educational level between urban and rural settlements.

INTER-KIBBUTZ INDUSTRIAL COOPERATION

Inter-Kibbutz industrial cooperation is based on a number of factors, of which the most important are: cooperation based on a division of production lines between Kibbutzim; cooperation based on manpower and capital investment; cooperation based on manpower alone; and cooperation based on sub-contracting.

Cooperation Based on a Division
of Production Lines Among Kibbutzim

All the Kibbutzim that are parties to an agreement of this kind are owners of independent industrial plants. This agreement lays down the division of production lines among the settlements so that each of them produces one part of the finished product.

One example of this arrangement is Michsaf. Michsaf markets cutlery (knives, spoons, and forks) through cooperation between two Kibbutzim, Urim and Nir Am. Both Kibbutzim lie in the south, north of Beersheba. Kibbutz Urim produces all Michsaf's knives and Nir Am produces the other items of cutlery and does all the packaging. If either of the Kibbutzim does not coordinate or falls behind in its commitments, both sides are affected.

A second example is the Dafna plastic products factory. This is a cooperative venture of three Kibbutzim in the north of the country. The original factory, called Dafna Shoes, is in Kibbutz Dafna and produces plastic shoes and boots, Kibbutz Ein Zivan produces plastic sandals called Dafna sandals and marketed by Dafna Shoes. Kibbutz Hulata produces Noah slippers marketed by Dafna Shoes.

A third example is the Netzer Sereni Industry. Five Kibbutzim from all parts of the country cooperate in this venture, which deals in the assembly of fire engines, trailers, and other transport vehicles. A large number of the parts of the final products are supplied by the Kibbutzim Ein Harod, Tel Yosef, Ashdod Yaakov, and Ramat David.

A fourth example is the Na'an Factory for sprinklers and irrigation equipment. There is an agreement of cooperation between the Na'an plant in Kibbutz Na'an and Kibbutz Gilgal, whick operates an assembly department for some of the equipment produced by Na'an.

Cooperation Based on Manpower and Capital Investment

This kind of cooperation is generally carried out in partnership between Kibbutzim in a project under one roof, on the grounds of one of the partners. Conditions for the formation of this kind of cooperation are geographic proximity of the Kibbutzim, similar or same origin of the population, and good social relationships between the neighboring Kibbutzim.

An example of this type of cooperation is the Hazorea Wood Industry. The Hazorea plant is in Kibbutz Hazorea and has been functioning for some 16 years. It started in partnership with a

private entrepreneur and with hired labor. In recent years the movement secretariat exerted pressure on Kibbutz Hazorea to cancel the
partnership with the private businessman and to employ less hired
labor in the plant. Kibbutz Hazorea therefore decided to set up an
inter-Kibbutz partnership with the neighboring Kibbutz Givat-Oz.
Kibbutz Hazorea holds two-thirds of the investment capital and manpower while Kibbutz Givat-Oz has one-third of each. Profits are
divided in the same proportion, two-thirds to Hazorea and one-third
to Givat Oz. The partnership with the private entrepreneur has been
dissolved. The movement secretariat fulfills the function of a con-
sulting and coordinating body which inspects agreements and arbitrates
in disputes among the partners in an industrial enterprise.

A second example is the Arad Plant. The Arad plant is in
Kibbutz Dalia, and produces water meters and delicate plastic parts
for industry. The plant has succeeded in developing an accurate water
meter which is in great demand both locally and abroad. In view of
market demands and the recommendation of the movement secretariat
it was decided to expand the plant by going into partnership with a
neighboring Kibbutz both in manpower and in capital investment.
Kibbutz Ramot Menashe agreed to enter into this partnership, and
some of its members travel daily to work in the plant in Kibbutz
Dalia. The service department of the Arad plant, which carries out
repairs on the clients' premises is to be set up in Kibbutz Ramot
Menashe. Ramot Menashe supplies 20 percent of the capital investment and manpower in the Arad plant in Kibbutz Dalia.

Inter-Kibbutz Cooperation Based on Manpower Alone

In this system of cooperation, the industrial plant is owned by
one of the Kibbutzim and members of a neighboring Kibbutz go to
work there. The neighboring Kibbutz only participates in the plant
insofar as manpower is concerned, and in return the workers are
paid wages and their Kibbutz is allocated a certain share of the
profits after deduction of profits on capital investment.

An example is the Nirim Electronics Israel plant. There is cooperation based on manpower between Kibbutz Nirim and Kibbutz
Magen in the Nirim Electronics Israel plant. Until 1967 each of these
Kibbutzim had an electronics factory. Kibbutz Magen's electronic
plant produced such items as radios and stereophonic sets. The
demands of the local market for electronic products for security
services and for agriculture are extensive; there is much less demand for electronic products in the entertainment field. This meant

too many workers in Magen and a shortage of manpower in Nirim. The
proximity of the two Kibbutzim and their good neighborly relations
have led to their temporary cooperation in manpower. They are considering merging the two plants in the future for the production of a
wide range of electronic products.

A second example is the Revadim Plant. Kibbutz Revadim and
Kibbutz Nachshon cooperate in manpower. The two Kibbutzim are
neighbors, and accepted their movement's recommendation to cooperate
in manpower in one plant which was set up on capital invested by
Kibbutz Revadim on its own grounds. The income of the plants is to
be shared between the member workers after deduction of returns on
Revadim's capital investment. This cooperation is planned to enable
one plant to be established in which members of Kibbutz Nachshon
can also specialize. After an experimental period, they will decide
if the markets and the returns on the investment justify adding more
production lines to the existing plant by setting up another finishing
plant in Kibbutz Nachshon, which will be run by those members
specializing in the finishing process in Revadim.

Cooperation Through Sub-Contracting

In this kind of cooperation the Kibbutz owner of an industrial
plant hands over its skills and reputation to an industrial plant set up
in another Kibbutz, enabling it to serve as a sub-contractor. The
agreement of cooperation enables the Kibbutz plant set up as a sub-
contractor to develop its own independent production of additional
articles on condition that they will not compete with the parent plant.

One example is the cooperation between Plastofile Hazorea Ltd.
and the Plastics Factory of Kibbutz Barkai. These two Kibbutzim
belong to the same movement and are at a distance of about 40 kilometers from each other. The Plastofile Hazorea factory produces
polyethylene for agriculture and packaging. It has succeeded in
marketing its goods both in Israel and abroad, and wishes to extend
its range of products. Kibbutz Barkai has agreed to set up a plastics
factory on its own grounds to produce 250 tons of goods for Plastofile
Hazorea Ltd., the raw material to be supplied by Plastofile Hazorea
Ltd. According to the agreement the products developed by Kibbutz
Barkai over and above this quota are to be different from those produced by Plastofile Hazorea Ltd., in order to avoid competition.

A second example is cooperation between Plason-Ma'agan
Michael and Teffen-Nachsholim. Ma'agan Michael and Nachsholim
are two neighboring Kibbutzim situated south of Haifa on the coastal

plain. The Plason factory is interested in expanding the scope of its
production, but because of Ma'agan Michael's limited manpower an
agreement was drawn up between Plason and Kibbutz Nachsholim to
set up a plastics factory in Nachsholim, Teffen, which is to produce
a certain quota for Plason. Raw material is to be supplied by Plason,
which will also provide the trademark and quality control. Teffen is
permitted to produce additional products provided they do not compete
with Plason products.

A third example is cooperation between the Plasim factory,
Merhavia, and the Terplex Plant, Reshafim. Plasim and Terplex
produce plastic irrigation products and equipment. The Terplex
factory supplies a fixed quota of goods for Plasim, working as a sub-
contractor of Plasim.

CONCLUSION

In conclusion, we can make the following statements: First,
agreements of cooperation in Kibbutz industry are generally based
on mutual trust between the Kibbutzim which are parties to the agreement. In the event of differences between the parties, the movement
secretariat acts as an arbitrator between the parties.

Second, the factory which joins the old established plant receives the rights to its trademark, skills, and so on, and in exchange
for these rights the veteran plant naturally receives appropriate compensation.

Third, if one of the sides is dissatisfied with the cooperation,
it may sever its connections at the end of the period of the agreement.

These factors determine the choice between alternative forms
of cooperation agreements:

1. The most convenient structure for industrial production.

2. The geographic distance between the Kibbutzim that are
parties to the cooperation agreement.

3. The composition of the population and the social relationships between the Kibbutzim that are parties to the agreement.

4. The security importance of the location of the Kibbutz.

5. The size of the industrial plant in relation to other branches
of the economy in the Kibbutz.

These cooperation agreements in industry solve part of the
present manpower problem, even though there is still hired labor
employed in most of the industrial plants. With regard to the future,
it would seem that the younger Kibbutzim which have suitable manpower
will agree to take part in various forms of cooperation in existing
Kibbutz industries.

There are three advantages inherent in regional industrial plants:

1. Regional industry is in a position to employ hired labor without affecting the Kibbutz society. Regional industry in its cooperative form can include both Kibbutz settlements and industrial workers from other settlements.

2. The merging of neighboring Kibbutz settlements in regional enterprises enables them to take maximum advantage of local talent. A concentration of large regional enterprises attracts experts, engineers, and executive personnel from outside to work in these plants.

3. Industrial bodies in large regions succeed in mobilizing capital and credit far more easily than small ones.

It may well be that these factors will lead from local cooperation in Kibbutz industry to regional and perhaps even inter-regional cooperation.

Maurice Konopnicki

The great diversity of the themes approached during the French-Israeli Conference on Rural Communities prohibits any generalizing. Some lessons can be learned, however. The results of some experiments show that the application of standard cooperative models for rural development is questionable. For the Third World, indeed, the problem is the development of traditional local forces, and indigenous and special programs adapted to particular circumstances.

The setting up of cooperatives has been for half a century the favorite instrument of agricultural policies in underdeveloped rural areas. Colonial administrations have made abundant use of them to control production and the peasant population. Planters and settlers have found in them an effective form of organizing their professional interests. Contemporary rural development and agrarian reform programs make widespread use of cooperatives because they see them as the only means of making their assistance to the peasantry an economic proposition by directing the largest possible number of small farmers towards commercial production and offering them a framework for economic and social participation. In the presence of a general revision of the policy of aid to the Third World it is surprising that, in a field of such social scope and one which deals with the great masses of underdeveloped populations, so few efforts at innovations are met with amongst the promoters of cooperatives.

Cooperation changes its meaning according to the contexts in which it operates. In countries of old, Western and individualistic civilizations, cooperation is a defense reaction against an economic and social system which has brought about the rupture between property and the forces of production. In African countries with collectivist traditions, on the other hand, it appears as an effort to free cooperators from the ascendancy of old collectivities and to develop personal profit through the economic emancipation of individuals.

The history of cooperation in the Third World is marked with failures. The very abundant literature devoted to it is as stirring when it deals with the future as it is depressing when speaking of the present and of the past. Cooperatives are only justifiable when they meet a real need and replace or compete with some chance of success with an inadequate or abusive private sector. Unfortunately, the regions where private initiative is not very active and where, consequently, the intervention of a cooperative would be especially necessary, are also those where agriculture is the least remunerative. Consequently there is a risk of leading to a situation in which private activity would take over what is economically sound, leaving to the cooperatives what is not.

One of the primary causes of the failure of cooperatives in the Third World is the fact that the fields of activity in which the members are competent do not coincide with technically and commercially complex agriculture. What can be efficiently organized by the cooperators is mostly not a paying proposition, whereas what does pay is uncontrollable. Consequently the primary cooperatives must increasingly become units of solidarity and mutual guarantee, whereas the more sophisticated activities must be concentrated at a higher level, that of the unions or federations of unions outside the scope of individual cooperators but remaining connected with them through the interplay of a system of elections. This plan seems still to be out of reach of the majority of developing countries.

The cooperative must operate efficiently. At the origin of most of the failures are found the same operational difficulties which are spread over the four levels of cooperation: the cooperators, the committees, the manager, and the tutelage authorities. It is easier to set up an association than to make traditional solidarity develop into cooperative solidarity. Compulsory cooperation always ends up by disconnecting the lower ranks from the higher, by stifling the former's initiatives, and by preventing their participation. The chief aim of cooperation should be: the material and social well-being of the farmers within independent associations for which they assume responsibility. Their aim is too often sacrificed to considerations of expediency and ideology. It would be preferable to concentrate on a few simple projects with real chances of success and to run efficiently some precooperative and cooperative organizations which will serve as an encouragement, an example, and a lesson.

One of the fundamental problems of European peasantry is the respective bargaining power of the various centers of economic decision. It is because their bargaining power remains slight that the farmers are defrauded of the results of their efforts; the level of agricultural prices reflects this inequality of power. Unless they manage to strengthen their own economic power, which they cannot do without accepting collective discipline, the peasantry will not be able to make headway and will be compelled, as in the past, to place themselves completely in the hands of public management authorities.

The solution will come through the setting up of peasant decision-making centers strong enough to carry sufficient weight in the daily bargaining which characterizes exchange activities. This remedy consists in recommending the systematic implanting in rural areas of institutions which industry has spontaneously used to consolidate its influence on the market and increase its profit-making capacity. The essential point is that the destinies of agriculture must be taken in hand by men who are from the country and are acquainted with its problems and can obtain a hearing for them. Aside from the setting up of this peasant force, there is hope for the farmers only in economic aid or in social welfare. In addition, emphasis must be given to the inevitable extension of village activities to the regional scale and, on the integration of agriculture, industry and services in the rural areas.

LIST OF CONFERENCE PARTICIPANTS

S. Assaf	Federation of Moshavim, Israel
M. Auge	Deputy Director, École Pratique des Hautes Études (EPHE), Paris
F. Baladier	Director of the Development Department of the Agricultural Training Association (AFPA), France
Y. Le Balle	University of Grenoble
C. Barberis	National Institute of Rural Sociology (INSOR), University of Rome, Italy
E. Ben-Raphael	Member of Kibbutz Hanita, Israel, Department of Sociology, Haifa University
A. Berler	Haifa University, Settlement Study Centre, Rehovot
M. Boulet	Adult Education, ENSSAA, Dijon, France
A. Daniel	Chairman, Department of Labor Studies, University of Tel Aviv
H. Desroche	Director, EPHE, Paris
Y. Don	Department of Economics, Bar-Ilan University, Israel
J. Eaton	School of Social Work, Haifa University, Israel
F. Elena (Diaz)	Director of A.E. Cooperative, Madrid, Spain
L. Ergan	Research Director, CELIB, Bretagne, France
H. De Farcy	Member of the Academy of Agriculture and of the Academy of Commercial Sciences, France
I. Fisera	Research Fellow of the National Scientific Research Center (CNRS), France
Z. Gat	Jewish Colonization Association (ICA), Israel
T. Guiart	Chairman of the Laboratory of Ethnology of the Musée de l'Homme, Paris, and Dean of the Faculty of Social Sciences, University René Descartes, Paris
P. Houée	Research Fellow, Social Research Foundation, France

For a few days the group of EPHE was joined by 15 members of the Cultural Promotion Group directed by Paul Houée and Guy Madiot, who added an agreeable Breton atmosphere to the group.

A. Kellerman	Department of Geography, Haifa University
M. Konopnicki	Department of Sociology, Haifa University
S. Koulytchizky	University of Bordeaux, France
Y. H. Landau	Haifa University, Settlement Study Centre, Rehovot
G. Lanneau	Chairman, Department of Behavioral and Education Sciences, University of Toulouse, France
M. Lebot	Rural Expert (CANA - ANCENIS), Bretagne, France
Y. Levi	Haifa University
Mrs H. Margulies	Settlement Study Centre, Rehovot
S. Molho	Settlement Study Centre, Rehovot
M. Martin	Rural Expert, Mene, Bretagne, France
S. Pohoryles	Tel Aviv University
F. Rambaud	EPHE, Paris
P. Raymackers	Director of the Bureau of Rural Program Organization, National University of Zaire
A. Rokach	Settlement Study Centre, Rehovot
H. Rosenfeld	Haifa University
A. Rozenman	Settlement Study Centre, Rehovot
M. Saltman	Department of Sociology, Haifa University
G. Sautter	EPHE, Paris
T. Shanin	Haifa University
O. Shapiro	Haifa University
Y. Sheffer	Haifa University, Member of Kibbutz Kfar Hachoresh
A. Sofer	Haifa University
D. Solomonica	Settlement Study Centre, Rehovot
P. Stahl	EPHE, Paris
S Stern	Haifa University
A. Szeskin	Ministry of Agriculture, Israel
R. Weitz	Haifa University; Head of Settlement Study Centre, Rehovot
A. Yassour	Haifa University, Member of Kibbutz Merhavia, Israel
Y. Yakir	Registrar of Cooperatives, Ministry of Labor Israel

LIST OF ADDITIONAL PAPERS
PRESENTED AT THE CONFERENCE
BUT NOT INCLUDED IN THE BOOK

Marc Auge	The Rural Illusion (Sociological and political constraints to rural development in the Ivory Coast)
Francois Baladier	Training for Micro-Regional Development
Corrado Barberis	Tourism and Rural Development in the Abruzzi Mountains
Michel Boulet	Micro-Regional Participation and Development
Joseph W. Eaton	When Cooperatives Succeed and Grow Old
F. Elena (Diaz)	Fifteen Years of Self-Development in the Zone of Mondragon
Louis Ergan	The "Country" in Bretagne
Joseph Fisera	Migration and Development (A Comparative Study in Socialist Economies)
Zvi Gat	Rural Development—The Israeli Model
Jean Guiart	Indigenous Development (The Case of Oceania)
Aaron Kellerman	Spatial Distribution of Inter-Village Centers in Israel
Serge Koulytchizky	Bargaining Power and Cooperative Concentration in Agriculture
Gaston Lanneau	A Psycho-Sociological Analysis of Agricultural Cooperation
Michel Martin	The Development Committee of Mene (Integrated Development of a Small Rural Region in the Bretagne
Paul Raymackers	Self-Development and Inter-Cooperation in the Marginal Savannas of Western Central Africa
Michael Saltman	Patterns of Cooperation Among the Kipsigis of Southwest Kenya
Gilles Sautter	Development of Secondary and Tertiary Activities in Rural Areas in Africa
Joseph Shepher	Kibbutz Members in Public Service
Arnon Sofer	Factors Limiting Regional Cooperation in the Western Jezreel Valley
Paul Henri Stahl	The Rumanian Traditional Village and the "Agricultural Collective Cooperatives"

YEHUDA H. LANDAU: Israel, Associate Professor, University
of Haifa, School of Social Work; member, Academic Council, Settlement Study Centre, Rehovot; engaged, since 1947, in integrated Rural
and Regional Development—research, teaching, planning, and implementation; various missions as Consultant to UNDP and OECD in
Europe, Asia, and Latin America; author and editor of articles and
books on rural development; M.Sc. Agriculture, Hochschule fuer
Bodenkultur, Vienna, Austria, and Hebrew University, Jerusalem,
1947.

MAURICE KONOPNICKI: Israel, Senior Lecturer, University
of Haifa; member, Academic Council, Settlement Study Centre,
Rehovot; Visiting Professor at several European Universities; Research Fellow at several Research Centers in Israel and Europe;
author of articles and books on economics and sociology of cooperation and on Israel Rural Development; Docteur en Sciences Com-
merciales, University of Liege, Belgium, 1967; first Belgian Frize
of Cooperation, 1968.

HENRI DESROCHE: France, Directeur d'Etudes at l'Ecole des
Hautes Etudes en Sciences Sociales, Sorbonne; director of the College
Coopératif, Paris; founder and director of "Archives Internationales
de Sociologies de la Coopération et du Développement"; various
missions as Visiting Professor and Consultant; author of articles and
books, mainly on cooperation and cooperatives; Docteur d'Etat -
lettres et Sciences Humaines.

PLACIDE RAMBAUD: France, Professor of Rural Sociology
at l'Ecole des Hautes Etudes en Sciences Sociales, Sorbonne; comparative research of social transformation of agricultural labor in
France, Romania and Israel; author of articles and books on Rural
Sociology; Doctor of Sociology.

YVES LE BALLE: France, coordinator of instruction in rural
economics, Faculty of Economic Sciences, University of Grenoble;
publications on agricultural labor in France and on collective agriculture in Yugoslavia; Docteur en Sciences Economiques, University of
Paris.

ELIEZER BEN-RAFAEL: Israel, member of Kibbutz Hanita; lecturer on Sociology, Hebrew University, Jerusalem; Research Fellow at Harvard University, 1974-75, and guest lecturer at the University of Massachusetts, 1975; published several papers on the sociology of the Kibbutz, of youth and of the student's revolution; Ph.D. in Sociology, Hebrew University, Jerusalem, 1973.

ABRAHAM DANIEL: Israel, Chairman, Department of Labor Studies, Tel Aviv University; author of articles and books on cooperatives; docteur en Sciences économiques, University of Paris, 1962

YEHUDA DON: Israel, Associate Professor of Economics, Bar-Ilan University; various professional assignments in Europe, India and Brazil; author of articles and research papers on cooperatives and economic topics; Ph.D., the London School of Economics, 1961.

HENRI DE FARCY: France, Professor, Catholic University, Paris; member, Agricultural Academy; member of the Academy of Commercial Sciences; consultant to international organizations; author of articles and books on Commerce and Economics; Doctorat in Geography, University of Lyon.

PAUL HOUÉE: France, Research Fellow at the CNRS (Centre National de la Recherche Scientifique); in charge of Training and Research in regional development at the Association de Formation et de Perfectionement Agricoles (AFPA), 1962-69; author of articles and books on rural development and cooperatives; Doctorat in Sociology, University of Poitiers.

MÉDARD LEBOT: France, in charge of promotion of cooperation at the Cooperative Agricole la Noelle Ancenis (CANA); graduate of the Ecole Superieure d'Agriculture, of Angers.

YAIR LEVI: Israel, Senior Lecturer, University of Haifa; Research Fellow and Lecturer at the Afro-Asian Institute for Cooperative and Labor Studies; 1968-1970, Project Director at the International Research Centre on Rural Cooperative Communities (CIRCOM), various missions to African and Asian countries; author of articles on rural cooperatives in developing countries and on cooperatives-trade unions relationship; docteur en sciences politiques, University of Liege, Belgium, 1969.

SAMUEL POHORYLES: Israel, Associate Professor in Rural Planning and Development, Tel Aviv University; director, Economic Survey and Advice Division of the Planning Center of the Ministry of Agriculture; member of FAO Rural Planning Experts Commission; member of an OAS Mission in Latin America; author of articles and books on rural development and planning of agriculture; Ph. D. in Economics and in Agriculture.

ARIEH L. SZESKIN: Israel, Head of Economic Research Section, Division of Economic Survey and Advice, Planning Centre, Ministry of Agriculture; author of articles on cooperatives and economic planning; docteur en sciences économiques, University of Paris.

RAANAN WEITZ: Israel, Professor, Regional Development, University of Haifa; Head, Settlement Study Centre, Rehovot; Head, Settlement Department, Jewish Agency for Israel; since 1938 engaged in comprehensive Rural and Regional Development, research, teaching, planning and implementation; Visiting Professor at Universities in Asia, Europe and Latin America; Consultant to various international agencies; author of articles and books on development problems and regional planning; Doctor of Science, University of Florence, Italy, 1937.

AVRAHAM YASSOUR: Israel, member of Kibbutz Merhavia; Senior Lecturer, Department of Political Science, University of Haifa; author of articles, research papers, and books on political philosophy and theory; doctorat, University of Paris, 1964.

RELATED TITLES
Published by
Praeger Special Studies

ACTION-ORIENTED APPROACHES TO REGIONAL DEVELOPMENT
PLANNING
Avrom Bendavid-Val and
Peter P. Waller

DEVELOPMENT REGIONS IN THE SOVIET UNION, EASTERN
EUROPE, AND CANADA
edited by Andrew F. Burghardt

MERCHANTS AS PROMOTERS OF RURAL DEVELOPMENT:
An Indian Case Study
Paul A. London

POLITICS AND DEVELOPMENT IN RURAL MEXICO:
A Study of Socio-Economic Modernization
Manuel L. Carlos

REGIONAL ECONOMIC ANALYSIS FOR PRACTITIONERS:
An Introduction to Common Descriptive Methods
(Revised Edition)*
Avrom Bendavid

TRADITIONAL ORGANIZATIONS AND ECONOMIC DEVELOPMENT:
Studies of Indigenous Cooperatives in Liberia
Hans Dieter Seibel and
Andreas Massing

*Also available in paperback as a PSS Student Edition